MW00897878

The
Prisoner's Hope
Personal
Bible
Genuine Hope

Newton R. Francis

ISBN 978-1-64140-370-2 (paperback)
ISBN 978-1-64140-371-9 (digital)

Copyright © 2018 by Newton R. Francis

All rights reserved. No part of this publication may be reproduced, distributed, or transmitted in any form or by any means, including photocopying, recording, or other electronic or mechanical methods without the prior written permission of the publisher. For permission requests, solicit the publisher via the address below.

Christian Faith Publishing, Inc.
832 Park Avenue
Meadville, PA 16335
www.christianfaithpublishing.com

All Scripture references are taken from the Authorized King James version.

Additional editorial supervision by Dr. Rambo.

Printed in the United States of America

"For thus saith the Lord of hosts; After the glory hath he sent me unto the nations which spoiled you: for he that toucheth you toucheth the apple of his eye."
Zechariah 2:8

I want to thank my heavenly "twin" brother, Kyle Toth, for being the first person to read this book and, most of all, for being such a skillful editor of the manuscript while preserving my unconventional style of writing. Brother Kyle, you truly understand me and our Father's heavenly culture, which I strive to pursue on this Earth.

Dedicated to Jesus Christ, Our Lord, Savior, and coming King.

God, you have given me an exceptional Mama, who
loves me and to whom I am eternally in love with.
Sister GG, you are the apple of my eyes.
You are too good to me.
To my siblings, I love you and miss you all.
Barry, you lovingly devoted so much of your
life to fill the vacuum I left behind.
Leo, I admire the Jesus in you.
Julieth, your album *Lend A Hand* is no doubt building
our Father's Kingdom. I cannot wait to hear it all.
Mother, even though you were a scared teenager, you gave me life.
Thanks for bringing me into this world.
I love you.
And I truly apologize for all the mistakes I have made in life.
I am saved now in Jesus' name.

Compiled and Written with the inspiration of the Holy Spirit.

"He was taken from prison and from judgment: and who shall declare his generation? for he was cut off out of the land of the living: for the transgression of my people was he stricken."

Isaiah 53:8

"As for thee also, by the blood of thy covenant I have sent forth thy prisoners out of the pit wherein is no water. Turn you to the strong hold, ye prisoners of hope: even today do I declare that I will render double unto thee."

Zechariah 9:11–12

This book contains the Word of God,
the primary authority for the prisoners'
hope and freedom.

Contents

Acknowledgments

Writing a book often requires bursts of inspiration along the way, from various source, places, and people. Often, there are too many people to acknowledge by name. So, to anyone I omitted, please know it was not intentional. Thank you to all of you!

I want to thank my good friend Dr. Rambo for letting *love* move him to be so instrumental in helping me to get this book ready for publishing.

I humbly would like to thank Antone Henshaw for his invaluable assistance in bringing this manuscript to fruition.

I salute Charles Sonntag, president and founder of the Incarcerated Veterans of America, Inc., the staff, and my fellow veterans who supported me in every way to accomplish writing this book. Your service to incarcerated veterans are admirable.

Special thanks to my caring friend Robert Miller for all his support and encouragements throughout the course of this writing. My friend, I consider you the best engineer and math tutor ever.

To my first draft typist, Vick, I am praying that you may regain your faith in Jesus. Thanks for all your assistance.

Special thanks to my Friday-night Bible study group, to whom I first revealed the creation of this book in August of 2014. You saints supported me with your prayers throughout my many sickly years—

when at times I could hardly walk, much less write. I am still in the process of mending to this day by God's help.

Many thanks to Dalbert Walker, director of Adult Distributed Education at Hobe Sound Bible College, and his staff for encouraging me to continue with my Bible college studies. I promise that I will complete my studies as soon as my health improves. Thanks also to American Bible Academy staff in Joplin, MO, who equipped me with sound Bible teachings. To everyone that sponsored my scholarship at ABA, I say thank you very much.

A big "thank you" to the congregation of the Church of the Reconciled at Rahway State Prison. There, for the past seven years, I worshiped with the finest saints under Rev. Dr. Larry Akins, along with a bundle of brilliant in-house pastors, preachers, and teachers too many to mention by name. All of you are deeply appreciated, admired, and loved.

I would like to give special tribute to all the churches, ministries, and volunteers who laid aside weekly their lives to come into this prison for fellowship with us. Ministries like Shilo Baptist Church; First Park Baptist Church, with Rev. McClendon; New Providence, with Rev. David Bryant, author of *Christ Is All*, a book that truly inspired me; Metro Community Church; and Free Indeed Ministries, with Brother Hardough, the "walking miracle cancer killa man." You are an inspiration to me. Thanks also to United Methodist; Trinity Temple; Calvary Chapel; and Full Circle Ministry, with our dear Brother Ulysses, whose gentleness and meekness has made him great as King David.

Special honor also to Rev. Morales and the Spanish Ministries, to whom I am forever indebted for their faithfulness to the Spanish community. Thanks to City of Refuge; House of God for the Nation; Church of God; United Brothers in Christ; New Jerusalem; Mission of Strength and Salvation; and Canaan Mission II. I cannot thank you all enough for the encouragement you conveyed.

A big thank you to Kenneth Copeland for taking from his own resources to help me pursue my Christian education. May God continue to bless you and your ministries

Special thanks also to the Catholic Ministries for all they do to enhance the faith of Jesus in me and many other incarcerated men.

Finally, I want to thank all the officers who inspired me over the years with their Christian example and bold confession of faith in the Lord Jesus Christ. Special thanks go out to Officer Reyes, a mighty woman of God in the faith, at Green Haven Correctional Facility in New York, and to Officer Reyes in New Jersey, the most caring, compassionate, and respectable man I ever encountered in uniform. Day by day, he exhibits 2 Samuel 23:3–4.

Introduction

Herein lies freedom for all men and women who are imprisoned physically and locked away from society and also for those who are under spiritual imprisonment, confined in bondage and captivity of sexual sins, lying, stealing, boozing, drugging, hating, coveting, bitterness, anger, fearfulness, stressing, unforgiveness, sickness and diseases in your bodies, rebelliousness, madness in your minds, physically or mentally abused, or engaged in gangs.

This is your handy Bible of selected verses, tailored to meet your specific needs wherever you are.

It provides you with the sure solution of God's Word if you will believe.

This book is filled with quick tips and insightful thoughts at the end of each page to alert your focus and attention to say, "Yes" or "No," as you receive God's freedom and hope.

My prayer is for all who are barricaded behind the bars of these sins to be loosed from their imprisonment through faith in Jesus holy Name. Amen, and so let it be by the power of the Most High God!

"... Christ in you, the hope of glory."
Glory to God!
Hallelujah!
Father, it is me again!

Creed

"Giving no offense in anything, that the ministry be not blamed:
But in all things approving ourselves as the ministers of God,
in much patience, in afflictions, in necessities, in distresses,
In stripes, in imprisonments, in tumults, in
labors, in watchings, in fastings;
By pureness, by knowledge, by longsuffering, by
kindness, by the Holy Ghost, by love unfeigned,
By the word of truth, by the power of God, by the amour
of righteousness on the right hand and on the left,
By honor and dishonor, by evil report and
good report, as deceivers and yet true;
As unknown, and yet well known; as dying, and,
behold we live; as chastened, and not killed;
As sorrowful, yet always rejoicing; as poor, yet making many
rich; as having nothing, and yet possessing all things."
2 Corinthians 6:3–9

CHAPTER 1

Prison

"The Spirit of the Lord is upon me because he hath anointed
me to preach the gospel to the poor; he hath sent me to heal the
broken-hearted, to preach deliverance to the captives, and recovery
of sight to the blind, to set at liberty them that are bruised,

To preach the acceptable year of the Lord."

St. Luke 4:18–19

Manna:

Are you ready for your freedom?

Yes _____

No _____

"And Joseph's master took him, and put him into
the prison, a place where the king's prisoners were
bound and he was there in the prison.
But the Lord was with Joseph, and showed him mercy, and
gave him favor in the sight of the keeper of the prison.
And the keeper of the prison committed to Joseph's
hand all the prisoners that were in the prison: and
whatsoever they did there, he was the doer of it.
The keeper of the prison looked not to anything that
was under his hand; because the Lord was with him, and
that which he did, the Lord made it to prosper."
Genesis 39:20–23

Manna:

Do you believe God is with you
and He will deliver you?

Yes _____

No _____

"And he put them in ward in the house of the captain of the
guard, into the prison, the place where Joseph was bound.
And the captain of the guard charged Joseph with them, and
he served them; and they continued a season in ward.
And they dreamed a dream both of them, each man
his dream in one night, each man according to the
interpretation of his dream, the butler and the baker of
the king of Egypt, which were bound in the prison.
But think on me when it shall be well with thee, and
shew kindness, I pray thee, unto me, and make mention
of me unto Pharaoh, and bring me out of this house.
For indeed I was stolen away out of the land of the
Hebrews: and here also have I done nothing that
they should put me into the dungeon."
Genesis 40:3–5, 14–15
Manna:
Do you know that man will fail you,
but God will not?

Yes _____

No _____

"Send one of you, and let him fetch your brother, and ye shall be kept in prison, that your words may be proved, whether there be any truth in you: or else by the life of Pharaoh surely ye are spies. If ye be true men, let one of your brethren be bound in the house of your prison: go ye, carry corn for the famine of your house."

Genesis 42:16, 19

Manna:

Did you know unbelief is like a famine or a disaster blocking the way of you receiving your miracle?

Yes _____

No _____

"But the Philistines took him, and put out his eyes, and brought him down to Gaza, and bound him with fetters of brass; and he did grind in the prison house.
And it came to pass, when their hearts were merry, that they said, Call for Samson, that he may make us sport.
And they called for Samson out of the prison house; and he made them sport: and they set him between the pillars."

Judges 16:21, 25

Manna:

Do you know, even if you feel you are chained between the pillars of injustice, there is still a miracle in God's Word for you?

Do you believe?

Yes _____

No _____

"And say, Thus saith the king, Put this fellow in the
prison, and feed him with bread of affliction and
water of affliction, until I come in peace."

1 Kings 22:27

Manna:

Living Manna shall you eat, and drink from the Rock Christ Jesus.

Will you share in His Living Manna?

Yes _____

No _____

"And the king of Assyria found conspiracy in Hoshea: for he had

sent messengers to So king of Egypt, and brought no present

to the king of Assyria, as he had done year by year: therefore

the king of Assyria shut him up, and bound him in prison.

And it came to pass in the seven and thirtieth year of the

captivity of Jehoiachin king of Judah, in the twelfth month, on

the seven and twentieth day of the month, that Evil-Merodach

king of Babylon, in the year that he began to reign, did lift

up the head of Jehoiachin king of Judah out of prison.

And changed his prison garments: and he did eat bread

continually before him all the days of his life."

2 Kings 17:4; 25:27, 29

Manna:

Oppression cannot stand in the way of God's supernatural power.

Do you agree?

Yes _____

No _____

"Then Asa was wroth with the seer, and put him in a prison house; for he was in a rage with him because of this thing. And Asa oppressed some of the people the same time. And say, Thus saith the king, Put this fellow in the prison, and feed him with bread of affliction and with water of affliction, until I return in peace."

2 Chronicles 16:10; 18:26

Manna:

The Word of God is your judgment of conviction declaring you free.

Will you agree?

Yes _____

No _____

"Palal the son of Uzai, over against the turning of the wall, and the tower which lieth out from the king's high house, that was by the court of the prison. After him Pedaiah the son of Parosh.
And from above the gate of Ephraim, and above the old gate, and above the fish gate, and the tower of Hananeel, and the tower of Meah, even unto the sheep gate: and they stood still in the prison gate.
So stood the two companies of them that gave thanks in the house of God, and I, and the half of the rulers with me."

Nehemiah 3:25, 12:39–40

Manna:

Having done everything you can to stand, stand even stronger with fortifications found in the promised Word in Jesus' name.

Will you accept this?

Yes _____

No _____

"Bring my soul out of prison, that I may praise
thy name: the righteous shall compass me about;
for thou shalt deal bountifully with me."

Psalm 142:7

Manna:

What God's Word has proclaimed,

it is for you to believe.

Agree with me?

Yes _____

No _____

"For out of prison he cometh to reign; whereas also
he that is born in his kingdom becometh poor."

Ecclesiastes 4:14

Manna:

You have a divine destiny to reign in this life.

Do you believe?

Yes _____

No _____

"And they shall be gathered together, as prisoners
are gathered in the pit, and shall be shut up in the
prison, and after many days shall they be visited.
To open blind eyes, to bring out the prisoners from the prison,
and them that sit in darkness out of the prison house.
But this is a people robbed and spoiled; they are all of them
snarled in holes, and they are hid in prison houses; they are for a
prey, and none delivereth; for a spoil, and none saith, Restore."
Isaiah 24:22; 42:7, 22
Manna:
Did you know Jesus came into the world to seek and
to save every prisoner and give him or her hope?
Yes, He came personally for you too.
Will you receive Him today?
Yes _____
No _____

"He was taken from prison and from judgment: and who shall declare his generation? For he was cut off out of the land of the living: for the transgression of my people was he stricken. The Spirit of the Lord God is upon me; because the Lord hath anointed me to preach good tidings unto the meek; he hath sent me to bind up the broken-hearted, to proclaim liberty to the captives, and the opening of the prison to them that are bound."

Isaiah 53:8; 61:1

Manna:

Jesus walked the crooked road of injustice to His death on the cross. The prophesized Word of God raised Him from the dead with power.

Is anything too hard for the Lord?

Yes _____

No _____

"The Lord hath made thee priest in the stead of Jehoiada the
priest, that ye should be officers in the house of the Lord,
for every man that is mad, and maketh himself a prophet,
that thou shouldest put him in prison, and in the stocks."
Jeremiah 29:26
Manna:
When God promotes you, no man can demote you.
"Humble yourselves therefore under the mighty hand
of God, that he may exalt you in due time."
Will you trust God?
Yes _____
No _____

"For then the king of Babylon's army besieged Jerusalem:
and Jeremiah the prophet was shut up in the court of
the prison, which was in the king of Judah's house.
So Hanameel mine uncle's son came to me in the court of
the prison according to the word of the Lord, and said unto
me, Buy my field, I pray thee, that is in Anathoth, which
is in the country of Benjamin: for the right of inheritance
is thine, and the redemption is thine; buy it for thyself.
Then I knew that this was the word of the Lord. And I gave the
evidence of the purchase unto Baruch the son of Neriah, the
son of Maaseiah, in the sight of Hanameel mine uncle's son,
and in the presence of the witnesses that subscribed the book of
purchase, before all the Jews that sat in the court of the prison."
Jeremiah 32:2, 8, 12
Manna:
Be bold and obey the Word of God.
Your dreams will come alive even in prison.
Will you be bold and obey?
Yes _____
No _____

"Moreover the word of the Lord came unto Jeremiah the second
time, while he was yet shut up in the court of the prison, saying.
Now Jeremiah came and went out among the
people: for they had not put him into prison.
Wherefore the princes were wroth with Jeremiah, and
smote him, and put him in prison in the house of Jonathan
the scribe: for they had made that the prison.
Moreover Jeremiah said unto king Zedekiah, What
have I offended against thy servants, or against
this people, that ye have put me in prison?
Then Zedekiah the king commanded that they should
commit Jeremiah into the court of the prison, and that
they should give him daily a piece of bread out of the
baker's street, until all the bread in the city were spent.
Thus Jeremiah remained in the court of the prison."
Jeremiah 33:1; 37:4, 15, 18, 21
Manna:
Do you know when you feed on God's righteousness,
He will provide for your every need?
Yes _____
No _____

"Then took they Jeremiah, and cast him into the dungeon of
Malchiah the son of Hammelech, that was in the court of the
prison: and they let down Jeremiah with cords. And in the dungeon,
there was no water, but mire: so Jeremiah sunk in the mire.
So he drew up Jeremiah with cords, and took him up out of the
dungeon: and Jeremiah remained in the court of the prison.
So Jeremiah abode in the court of the prison until the day that
Jerusalem was taken: and he was there when Jerusalem was taken."

Jeremiah 38:6, 13, 28

Manna:

Your struggles may seem endless, but rest assured God can lift you
out of the dungeon's mire-clay, and set your feet on solid ground.

If you receive this, say Amen!

Yes _____

No _____

"Even they sent, and took Jeremiah out of the court

of the prison, and committed him unto Gedialiah the

son of Ahikam the son of Shaphan, that he should

carry him home: so he dwelt among the people.

Now the word of the Lord came unto Jeremiah, while he was

shut up in the court of the prison, saying, Go and speak . . ."

Jeremiah 39:14–16

Manna:

"Behold, I am the Lord, the God of all flesh:

is there anything too hard for me?"

"Go and speak . . ."

Be bold.

Confess your miracle.

Will you?

Yes _____

No _____

"Then he put out the eyes of Zedekiah; and the king of
Babylon bound him in chains, and carried him to Babylon,
and put him in prison till the day of his death.
And it came to pass in the seven and thirtieth year of the
captivity of Jehoiachin king of Judah, in the twelfth month, in
the five and twentieth day of the month, that Evil-Merodach
king of Babylon in the first year of his reign lifted up the head of
Jehoiachin king of Judah, and brought him forth out of prison.
And changed his prison garments: and he did continually
eat bread before him all the days of his life."
Jeremiah 52:11, 31, 33
Manna:
God is able to transform your circumstances from death to life,
from blind to sight, from lost to found, from salvation to glory,
from rags to the abundant life, from prison to the palace.
Can you see it coming for yourself?
Yes _____
No _____

"Now when Jesus had heard that John was cast
into prison, he departed into Galilee.
Agree with thine adversary quickly, while thou art in the way with
him; lest at any time the adversary deliver thee to the judge, and
the judge deliver thee to the officer, and thou be cast into prison."
St. Matthew 4:12; 5:25
Manna:
Prioritize your agreement with God's Word, and then your
argument with your adversary will reap your desired will.
Agree?
Yes _____
No _____

"Now when John had heard in the prison the

works of Christ, he sent two of his disciples.

For Herod had laid hold on John, and bound him, and put

him in prison for Herodias' sake, his brother Philip's wife.

And he sent, and beheaded John in the prison."

St. Matthew 11:12; 14:3, 10

Manna:

When Jesus is the fountain of your life,

He illuminates your path, and in His glistering

light you shall see light to navigate the dark pitfalls of life.

Take hold of this.

Will you?

Yes _____

No _____

"And he would not: but went and cast him into
prison, till he should pay the debt.
Naked, and ye clothed me: I was sick, and ye visited
me: I was in prison, and ye came unto me.
Or when saw we thee sick, or in prison, and came unto thee?"
St. Matthew 18:30; 25:36, 39
Manna:
God will never leave you nor forsake you. The
spotlight of heaven is shining on you wherever you
may be—even in prison, or on a sick bed.
Will you open your heart to Jesus today?
Yes _____
No _____

"I was a stranger, and ye took me not in:

Naked, and ye clothed me not: sick, and

in prison, and ye visited me not.

Then shall they also answer him, saying, Lord, when saw

we thee an hungered, or athirst, or a stranger, or naked,

or sick, or in prison, and did not minister unto thee."

St. Matthew 25:43–44

Manna:

God knows your difficult situations and will

design miracles to answer those needs.

Your life was customized prior to your existence.

What God has designed for your life can

never fail. It is supernatural.

Will you trust Him?

Yes _____

No _____

"Now after that John was put in prison, Jesus came into
Galilee, preaching the gospel of the kingdom of God.
For Herod himself had sent forth and laid hold upon
John, and bound him in prison for Herodias' sake,
his brother Philip's wife: for he had married her.
And immediately the king sent an executioner, and commanded his
head to be brought: and he went and beheaded him in the prison."
St. Mark 1:14; 6:17, 27
Manna:
The divine supernatural prophecy of a person's life
can never be changed, altered, or derailed.
God has spoken.
The Lord giveth and the Lord taketh away.
Will you praise His name?
Yes _____
No _____

"Added yet this above all, that he shut up John in prison.
When thou goest with thine adversary to the magistrate, as
thou art in the way, give diligence that thou mayest be delivered
from him; lest he hale thee to the judge, and the judge deliver
thee to the officer, and the officer cast thee into prison."

St. Luke 3:20; 12:58

Manna:

Do not allow your sins to take you to trial before the throne of God.

Plead your case at the foot of Jesus' cross.

His blood paid all your debts in full.

It is miraculous.

Do you believe this?

Yes _____

No _____

"And he said unto him, Lord, I am ready to go
with thee, both into prison, and to death.
Who for a certain sedition made in the city,
and for murder, was cast into prison.
And he released unto them him that for sedition
and murder was cast into prison, whom they had
desired; but he delivered Jesus to their will."
St. Luke 22:33; 23:19, 25
Manna:
Jesus Christ is the greatest name in the universe.
He is the master key for every prison lock.
No prisoner is beyond the reach for His mercy.
Jesus even knew Barabbas' prison number.
He died for everyone. That is love.
Do you know His name can pop open your lock?
It is the greatest prison swap ever.
Yes _____
No _____

"For John was not yet cast into prison."

John 3:24

Manna:

Hope called into action your faith. Remove the cloud of
imprisonment, and vitalize energy within you, readying you to be
an overcomer who will spark fire in other prisoners of hope's souls.
God Teflon-coated us for whatever may come our way in life.

Are you a prisoner of hope?

Yes _____

No _____

"And laid their hands on the apostles, and

put them in the common prison.

But the angel of the Lord by night opened the prison

doors, and brought them forth, and said,

Go, stand and speak in the temple to the

people all the word of this life."

Acts 5:18–20

Manna:

Miracles are pre-packaged by God.

They are all wrapped in his Word.

Your faith opens them.

Angels can perform them.

Will you believe God for the impossible today?

Yes _____

No _____

"And when they heard that, they entered into the temple early in the morning, and taught. But the high priest came, and they that were with him, and called the council together, and all the senate of the children of Israel, and sent to the prison to have them brought.

But when the officers came, and found them not in the prison, they returned, and told.

Saying, the prison truly found we shut with all safely, and the keepers standing without before the door: but when we had opened, we found no man within.

Then came one and told them, saying, Behold, the men whom ye put in prison are standing in the temple, and teaching the people."

Acts 5:21–25

Manna:

Prisoners of hope take all the limits off God.

Hope is a picture that you frame with your mind.

Then the impossible becomes possible.

Are you ready for a miracle?

Yes _____

No _____

"As for Saul, he made havoc of the church, entering into every
house, and hailing men and women committed them to prison."

Acts 8:3

Manna:

A tribute to the women who are prisoners of hope:

Jesus' heart of compassion is forever open to you.

The connection is special.

He was born of a virgin mother.

"Blessed art thou among women . . ."

His first miracle of turning water into wine

was in obedience to His mother.

". . . Whatsoever he saith unto you, do it."

The first to evangelize His gospel was the messed-up

woman at the well. "Come, see a man, which told me

all things that ever I did: Is not this the Christ?"

The only person to ever wash, kiss, and anoint Jesus' feet

was another messed up woman who washed them with her

tears, and dried them with her hair in a rich man's house.

". . . Her sins, which are many, are forgiven; for she loved much . . ."

This is the only woman Jesus builds a memorial for with His Word.
"Verily I say unto you, Wheresoever this gospel shall be
preached throughout the whole world, this also that she
hath done shall be spoken of for a memorial of her."
It was a woman's wailing over her brother's death which
overcame the Savior with uncommon compassion—
the only time Scripture records, "Jesus wept."
The first with the news of His resurrection was a woman of
great hope and faith like you. God is no respecter of persons.
Expect angels to appear to you as a prisoner of hope—
you are highly favored of the Lord. Amen!
Deeply loved, and marked for a miracle. Be
loosed from your imprisonment.
Will you receive this?
Yes _____
No _____

"And when he had apprehended him, he put him in prison, and delivered him to four quaternions of soldiers to keep him; intending after Easter to bring him forth to the people. Peter therefore was kept in prison: but prayer was made without ceasing of the church unto God for him. And when Herod would have brought him forth, the same night Peter was sleeping between two soldiers, bound with two chains: and the keepers before the door kept the prison. And, behold, the angel of the Lord came upon him, and a light shined in the prison: and he smote Peter on the side, and raised him up, saying, Arise up quickly. And his chains fell off from his hands. But (Peter) he, beckoning unto them with the hand to hold their peace, declared unto them how the Lord had brought him out of the prison. And he said, Go show these things unto James, and to the brethren. And he departed, and went into another place."

Acts 12:4–7, 17

Manna:

A praying church attracted an atmosphere of miracles and supernatural intervention for the prisoners of hope.

Will you pray without ceasing?

Yes _____

No _____

"And when they had laid many stripes upon them, they cast
them into prison, charging the jailer to keep them safely.
Who, having received such a charge, thrust them into the
inner prison, and made their feet fast in the stocks.
And at midnight Paul and Silas prayed, and sang
praises unto God: and the prisoners heard them.
And suddenly there was a great earthquake, so that the
foundations of the prison were shaken: and immediately all
the doors were opened, and every one's bands were loosed.
And the keeper of the prison awaking out of his sleep, and seeing
the prison door open, he drew out his sword, and would have
killed himself, supposing that the prisoners had been fled."

Acts 16:23–27

Manna:

Your worship can create earthquakes of miracles
wherever there is a need in your life.

God lives in your worship.

Worship God!

Will you?

Yes _____

No _____

"And the keeper of the prison told this saying
to Paul, The magistrates have sent to let you go:
now therefore depart, and go in peace.
But Paul said unto them, They have beaten us openly
uncondemned, being Romans, and have cast us into
prison; and now do they thrust us out privily? Nay verily;
but let them come themselves and fetch us out.
And they went out of the prison, and entered into
the house of Lydia: and when they had seen the
brethren, they comforted them, and departed."

Acts 16:36–37, 40

Manna:

The lives of the prisoners of hope are built with the war-
room materials of: faith, prayer, fasting, love, and worship,
custom-made to experience days of heaven on earth.

Will you give God your all today?

Yes _____

No _____

"Which thing I also did in Jerusalem: and many of the saints did I shut up in prison, having received authority from the chief priests; and when they were put to death, I gave my voice against them."

Acts 26:10

Manna:

Prisoners of hope, God can reverse that

verdict announced against you.

He can lose you from that cursed sentence pronounced over your life through the hope in which you stand, and set you free.

"Behold, I am the Lord, the God of all flesh:

is there anything too hard for Me?"

Do you embrace this?

Yes _____

No _____

"By which also he went and preached unto the spirits in prison."

1 Peter 3:19

Manna:

Jesus was dragged through the prison halls of injustice, railroaded with the collaboration of false witnesses all the way to the cross, and to every depth of imprisonment He went physically and spiritually to preach unto the spirits in prison. Not even death could quiet Him, or stop His love for *us*.

Will you receive this love?

Yes _____

No _____

"Fear none of those things which thou shalt suffer: behold, the devil shall cast some of you into prison, that ye may be tried; and ye shall have tribulation ten days: be thou faithful unto death, and I will give thee a crown of life."

Revelation 2:10

Manna:

The Word of God is the primary authority governing your future. Nothing can stop you when you put your faith in Jesus and believe God to His Word.

"God is not a man, that he should lie; neither the son of man, that he should repent: hath he said, and shall he not do it? or hath he spoken, and shall he not make it good?"

Do you believe His Word?

Yes _____

No _____

"And when the thousand years are expired,

Satan shall be loosed out of his prison."

Revelation 20:7

Manna:

Prisoners of hope, pack up all your failures of mental, spiritual,

physical, and intellectual imprisonment, including all sicknesses,

diseases, poverty, fears, unbelief, doubts, addictions, gangs—

bondages and prison sentences, and send all this stuff back

to Satan in his prison in the pits of hell where they blond.

This is his baggage.

Jesus Christ set us free from all these bondages of imprisonment.

You are free!

Receive it?

Yes _____

No _____

CHAPTER 2

Prisons

"But before all these, they shall lay their hands on you, and
persecute you, delivering you up to the synagogues, and into
prisons, being brought before kings and rulers for my name's sake."

St. Luke 21:12

Manna:

All they that lay their hands on you shall not prevail for long.
All they that persecute you, delivering you to synagogues
and into prisons, bringing you before officials and
rulers for our Lord's name sake, shall not prevail.
Prisoners of hope, here is what God's Word commanded
to prevail in your lives when you received it: "Therefore
let no man glory in men. For all things are yours; whether
Paul or Apollos, or Cephas or the world, or life, or death,
or things present, or things to come. All are yours.
And you are Christ's, and Christ is God's."
Will you believe this, and receive it?

Yes _____

No _____

"And I persecuted this way unto the death, binding and
delivering into prisons both men and women."

Acts 22:4

Manna:

The spirit of prosecution has been raising havoc on the
innocent throughout the history of the human race.
Dishing out the penalty of injustice to men and women,
hauling them off to prisons, death row, and death.
Not even the innocent Son of God was exempt from
the evil hands of injustice—he was arrested, prosecuted,
and sentenced to die on Calvary's cross.

Yes, He was.

"And moreover I saw under the sun the place of
judgment, that wickedness was there; and the place
of righteousness; that iniquity was there."

But I have good news!

Prisoners of hope, Jesus rose from the dead with
divine supernatural uncommon justice for you.

Will you receive this justice?

Yes _____

No _____

"Are they ministers of Christ?

(I speak as a fool) I am more; in labors more abundant, in stripes

above measure, in prisons more frequent, in deaths oft."

2 Corinthians 11:23

Manna:

Your obedience to the purpose of Christ in your life in the midst

of adversities is living proof which gives validity to your calling,

trust, and hope in God's unfailing promises as prisoners of hope.

"All the days of the afflicted are evil: but he that

is of a mercy heart hath a continual feast."

Wisdom speaks!

Can you see your present mess is just a rest

in preparation for your best?

Yes _____

No _____

CHAPTER 3

Prisoner

"Let the sighing of the prisoner come before thee; according to the
greatness of thy power preserve thou those that are appointed to die.
To hear the groaning of the prisoner; to lose
those that are appointed to death."
Psalm 79:1; 102:20
Manna:
The Word of God is the prisoner's hope. It is the
constitution of your existence. Open your mouth
and frame your world according to His Word.
God spoke worlds into existence with these same Words.
Even if you are sitting on death row today, death
row is not the anchor of your soul.
Jesus is.
God can snatch you from the jaws of defeat and death. You can
wreck the devil's plans against your life today, by just believing God.
Will you?
Yes _____
No _____

"Now at that feast the governor was wont to release
unto the people a prisoner, whom they would.
And they had then a notable prisoner, called Barabbas."
St. Matthew 27:15–16
Manna:
My fellow prisoners of hope rely not on your petitions before
the governor of the states in which you are imprisoned.
But rather, rely on your petitions before the Superior Governor
of all governors of states: The Lord Jesus Christ who presides
justly in loving mercy and grace without the influences of
others, and will not release the wicked for the righteous.
Will you appeal to the
Matthew 2:6 Governor today?
Yes _____
No _____

"Now at that feast he released unto them one

prisoner, whomsoever they desired."

Mark 15:6

Manna:

The desires of men are not always the desires of God.

Justice is often upside-down in this world for prisoners of hope.

But in the world to come, justice will be down-side up.

"Many seek the ruler's favor; but every man's

judgment cometh from the Lord."

Where is your judgment coming from?

Is it the Lord?

Yes _____

No _____

"So he took him, and brought him to the chief captain, and said, Paul the prisoner called me unto him, and prayed me to bring this young man unto thee, who hath something to say unto thee."

Acts 23:18

Manna:

Paul was a prisoner of hope who recognized
God's value in a young man's message.
It is God's pleasure to use our young men. So do not stand
in their way, as Rev. Larry Akins would say. Amen!
Do you remember the young man Joseph and his dreams?
How about Samson, Jeremiah, Daniel, Shadrach, Meshach,
and Abednego. Not to mention young Timothy, and John
the Baptist; young precursors all with a message.
". . . I am young, and ye are very old; wherefore I was afraid,
and darest not show you mine opinion. I said, Days should
speak, and a multitude of years should teach wisdom. But
there is a spirit in man: and the inspiration of the Almighty
giveth them understanding. Great men are not always
wise: neither do the aged understand judgment."
Do you believe this?
Yes _____
No _____

"For it seemeth to me unreasonable to send a prisoner,

and not withal to signify the crimes laid against him.

And it came to pass, that after three days Paul called the chief of

the Jews together: and when they were come together, he said

unto them, Men and brethren, though I have committed nothing

against the people, or customs of our fathers, yet was I delivered

prisoner from Jerusalem unto the hands of the Romans."

Acts 25:27; 28:17

Manna:

Thus saith the Holy Ghost to you prisoners

of hope, crushed by injustice.

You may have been shuffled from one jurisdiction to another on

baseless, false accusations. But be of good cheer and courage.

The High Court of heaven's divine grace has ruled

over your cause by the blood of Jesus.

You have been delivered from the Devil's

jurisdiction of sin and death.

Will you receive your defense?

Yes _____

No _____

"For this cause I Paul, the prisoner of Jesus Christ for you Gentile.

I therefore, the prisoner of the Lord, beseech you that ye

walk worthy of the vocation wherewith ye are called."

Ephesians 3:1; 4:1

Manna:

Prisoners of hope are prisoners of Jesus Christ inspired

by the Holy Spirit to walk worthy of the vocation

called by God, as it is written in the Holy Bible.

Scripture is the cultural expression and doctrinal tradition of

Heaven. It is what forms who we are, or what we become. The

Scripture is the language of Heaven. Your belief system is built on

what you hear, and what you believe. Whose voice are you hearing?

Whose advice are you following?

God has called you. Will you call Him back?

"Call unto me, and I will answer thee, and show thee

great and mighty things, which thou knowest not."

Will you call on Him today?

Yes _____

No _____

"Be not thou therefore ashamed of the testimony of our Lord, nor of me his prisoner: but be thou partaker of the afflictions of the gospel according to the power of God."

2 Timothy 1:8

Manna:

Behold the sparkle of Christ love in her eyes.

His face reflects Christ grace and humble majesty.

Purged of self and unashamed of their brothers in bonds, these two noble saints weekly share in the affliction of the everlasting gospel of Jesus Christ, bracing the scorns and rejections, they face with the meekness of Christ's Spirit to come into prison, and share the true Light of Christ's love with us.

Bro. Wilson and sister Dian are two of the countless saints who embrace the stigmatization of prisoners of hope affiliation and "hazard their lives for the name of our Lord Jesus Christ." You are both eternally loved.

Will you join them today?

Yes _____

No _____

"Paul, a prisoner of Jesus Christ, and Timothy our brother,
unto Philemon our dearly beloved, and fellow-laborer.
Yet for love's sake I'd rather beseech thee, being such an one
as Paul the aged, and, now also a prisoner of Jesus Christ."

Philemon 1, 9

Manna:

His love is in an abundant unlimited supply. Shed abroad
in the prisoners of hope's hearts by the Holy Ghost.
So for "love's sake" God is no respecter of person. For
"love's sake" His eyes are upon you. And for "love's sake"
His goodness and mercy shall pursue you daily.

Did you hear? For "love's sake."

"The Lord hath appeared of old unto me, saying, Yea,
I have loved thee with an everlasting love: therefore
with loving kindness have I drawn thee."

For "love's sake", will you receive Jesus Christ
right now as your Savior and Lord?

Yes _____

No _____

CHAPTER 4

Prisoners

"And Joseph's master took him, and put him into
the prison, a place where the king's prisoners were
bound: and he was there in the prison.
And the keeper of the prison committed to Joseph's
hand all the prisoners that were in the prison; and
whatsoever they did there, he was the doer of it."
Genesis 39:20, 22
Manna:
Jesus can change the molecular structure of your entire life in
the blink of an eye right now the same way He changed the
molecular structure of water into wine, and magnify your life to
vintage proportion by His Spirit so unusual and uncommon that
everyone will know that God is of a truth at work in your life.
"Whatsoever He saith unto you, do it."
Will you?
Yes _____
No _____

"And when king Arad the Canaanite, which dwelt in the south,
heard tell that Israel came by the way of the spies; then he
fought against Israel, and took some of them prisoners."

Numbers 21:1

Manna:

Prisoners of hope are blood-bought covenant children of God.
So from the moment you say, yes to Jesus, all the
promises and blessings of God are activated in your
life, and enforced by the Holy Ghost with power.
And no devil in hell can derail this even if you are taken
prisoners on the journey to your promised land. Amen!
"For all the promises of God in him are yea, and in
him Amen, unto the glory of God by us."
If you receive this, will you say Amen?

Yes _____

No _____

"There the prisoners rest together; they hear

not the voice of the oppressor."

Job 3:18

Manna:

There is a place in Jesus Christ where the prisoners of hope can

find rest, and bury the voice of their oppressor once and for all.

Seal off your life in the world of His Word.

"Let us therefore fear, lest, a promise being left us of entering

into his rest, any of you should seem to come short of it.

For unto us was the gospel preached, as well as unto them: but the

word preached did not profit them, not being mixed with faith in

them that heard it. For we which have believed do enter into rest."

Do you believe Christ is your rest?

Yes _____

No _____

"For the Lord heareth the poor, and despiseth not his prisoners.

Which executeth judgment for the oppressed,

which giveth food to the hungry.

The Lord looseth the prisoners."

Psalm 69:33; 146:7

Manna:

Prisoners of hope, keep praying: God is hearing you.

I can feel the Holy Ghost's vibration breaking forth like

on the day of Pentecost, obliterating your prison chains,

and all the plans of those who oppose your freedom.

"And it shall come to pass, that before they call, I will

answer; and while they are yet speaking, I will hear."

Are you ready to trust God to supply all your needs?

Yes _____

No _____

"Without me they shall bow down under the
prisoners, and they shall fall under the slain.
For all this his anger is not turned away,
but his hand is stretched out still.
That made the world as a wilderness, and destroyed the cities
thereof; that opened not the house of his prisoners?"
Isaiah 10:4; 14:17
Manna:
Without God, injustice would know no limits. Without
God, there would be no hope for the prisoners of
hope. Without Jesus, we can do nothing.
"If thou seest the oppression of the poor, and violent
perverting of judgment and justice in a province,
marvel not at the matter: for he that is higher than the
highest regardeth; and there be higher than they."
Be patient therefore, and wait on the Lord.
His hand is stretched out to free you.
But know, God is not on your deadline, or your timeline. He is
on your lifeline to bring you to His grand time. Will you wait?

Yes _____

No _____

"So shall the king of Assyria lead away the Egyptians prisoners,
and the Ethiopians captives, young and old, naked and barefoot,
even with their buttocks uncovered to the shame of Egypt.
And they shall be gathered together, as prisoners are
gathered in the pit, and be shut up in the prison,
and after many days shall they be visited."
Isaiah 20:4; 24:22
Manna:
How can we thank our Savior enough for subjecting
Himself to the likes of us prisoners of hope?
Young and old relate. We bear our own humiliation:
paraded naked and barefoot; with our buttocks
exposed to the indignities of the prison guards.
Shut up and locked down, but heaven's grace is wide open to *us*.
We cannot be stripped of our hope, purpose,
and glorious dignity. Amen!
Do you know how much Jesus loves you?
Yes _____
No _____

"To open the blind eyes, to bring out the prisoner from the prison, and them that sit in darkness out of the prison house. That thou mayest say to the prisoners, Go forth; to them that are in darkness, Shew yourselves. They shall feed in the ways, and their pastures shall be in all high places."

Isaiah 42:7; 49:9

Manna:

Prisoners of hope, thus saith the Lord: Your day of deliverance has come. Blind eyes will be open, prisoners set free, light shines in darkness, and the gospel flood gates open to your hearts. You will eat the finest now. Your heaviness has rolled away. Just look at that burden rolling down the hill to the pits of hell—crushing old Satan. Now let the Word germinate in your spirit, and elevate hope in you. You have seeds of greatness in you. Revive your dreams again.

You are a bearer of precious cargo.

"But we have this treasure in earthen vessels, that the excellency of the power may be of God, and not of us." Amen! Hallelujah!

It is supernatural.

Right?

Yes _____

No _____

"To crush under his feet all the prisoners of the earth."

Lamentation 3:34

Manna:

Prisoners of hope, "It is of the Lord's mercies that we are
not consumed, because his compassions fail not.
They are new every morning: great is thy faithfulness.
The Lord is my portion, saith my soul;
therefore, I will hope in him."
God did not create us to be crushed under
the feet of our adversaries.
Jesus was wounded for our transgressions, bruised for our
iniquities. He borne our grief and carried our sorrows
all the way to the cross—where they were crucified
and crushed under the wrath of God's feet.
And now, behold, we have been given power and authority
by Jesus Christ to crush devils and demons under our feet.
Is the adversary under your feet?

Yes _____

No _____

"As for thee also by the blood of the covenant, I have sent
forth thy prisoners out of the pit wherein is no water.
Turn ye to the stronghold, ye prisoners of hope: even today
do I declare that I will render double unto thee."
Zechariah 9:11–12
Manna:
If you have ears to hear, hear this. If you have eyes to see, read
this. If you have a mouth to speak, speak this. If you have
a mind to think, ponder this. If you have a heart to receive,
grab this. Take hold of it. Let it not go: for it is your life.
"Take fast hold of instruction."
The Bible is the primary authority of your
life. Its' superiority is unmatchable.
33 times this superior Holy Book calls your attention to instruction.
"Turn ye to the stronghold ye prisoners of hope."
Instruction! Turn or burn.
Read this book. The Prisoners' Hope Bible.
"Blessed is he that readeth." God promised.
Will you receive God's instructions?
Yes _____
No _____

"And at midnight Paul and Silas prayed, and sang

praises unto God: and the prisoners heard them.

And the keeper of the prison awaking out of his sleep, and seeing

the prison doors open, he drew out his sword, and would have

killed himself, supposing that the prisoners had been fled."

Acts 16:25, 27

Manna:

Here is one of the 8 examples I see of Scripture where

prisoners of hope must exercise their faith to engage

the supernatural, and experience the move of God's

miraculous power in their situations and life.

God lives in our praise. And faith rejoices His heart with pleasure.

"But without faith it is impossible to please him: for he

that cometh to God must believe that he is, and that

he is a rewarder of them that diligently seek him."

Will you follow the example of Scripture to pray and

praise God in all situations instead of complaining?

Yes _____

No _____

"And when it was determined that we should sail into
Italy, they delivered Paul and certain other prisoners unto
one named Julius, a centurion of Augustus' band.
And the soldiers' counsel was to kill the prisoners,
lest any of them should swim out, and escape.
And when we came to Rome, the centurion delivered the
prisoners to the captain of the guard: but Paul was suffered
to dwell by himself with a soldier that kept him."
Acts 27:1, 42; 28:16

Manna:

Prisoners of hope, when all is said and done, you may
find yourself all alone in a rented home under parole
supervision. But you can rest assured the Holy Spirit is like
an armed soldier sent from God to keep you. Amen!
You have endured the rugged stormy seas of life, swam
the toilsome waters of brokenness, while the cruel waves
of life's troubles sought to kill you. You have escaped by
the blood of the Lamb. Now freedom is in sight.

Can you see it?

Yes _____

No _____

CHAPTER 5

Captive

"And when Abram heard that his brother was taken captive,
he armed his trained servants, born in his own house, three
hundred and eighteen, and pursued them unto Dan.
And all their wealth, and all their little ones, and their wives
took they captive, and spoiled even all that was in the house."
Genesis 14:14; 34:29

Manna:

The need for us to prevail over captivity today is
warranted more than ever. It is urgent.
As prisoners of hope we must reverse the spoiling
and plundering of our lives, and families, and bring
an end to captivity, and restore stability.
Now hear this. You will never have what God gave you. You
will only have what you are willing to receive. "According as
his divine power hath given unto us all things that pertain
unto life and godliness, through the knowledge of him
that hath called us to glory and virtue. Whereby are given
unto us exceeding great and precious promises: that by
these you might be partakers of the divine nature . . ."
Will you believe and receive God's Word?

Yes _____

No _____

"And it came to pass, that at midnight the Lord smote all the firstborn in the land of Egypt, from the firstborn of Pharaoh that sat on his throne unto the firstborn of the captive that was in the dungeon; and all the firstborn of cattle."

Exodus 12:29

Manna:

Prisoners of hope, do not limit God by thinking your situation is hopeless. Remember how God brought Israel out of Egypt.

That was truly Grace!

When it comes to you: He will go to any measure to deliver you, and set you free from all captivity. If He has to disturb the cradles of man, and beast, and rattle the hearts of the powerful to bring you out. He will.

God is a midnight liberator for the afflicted and marginalized.

Do not ever limit your God.

"Yea, they turned back and tempted God, and limited the Holy One of Israel."

Do you have any limits on God?

Yes _____

No _____

"Nevertheless the Kenite shall be wasted, until
Asshur shall carry thee away captive."
Numbers 24:22
Manna:
Consider the grace of God bestowed upon us prisoners
of hope. No longer are we marked to be wasted, or
be carried away captive to pine away in despair.
Christ Jesus has long spoiled wasting and captivity at the cross.
With all limits removed off of God, we
received restoration in His Son.
Take what God has given you.
Take eternal life, take your freedom.
Take your healing, take your peace.
Take your joy, take your wealth.
Take contentment too—You will need it.
Yes, take all the blessings of God *given*.
Now see His voice in His Words of *truth*.
"And I will restore to you the years that the locust
hath eaten, the cankerworm, and the palmerworm,
my great army which I sent among you."
Do you believe this?
Yes _____
No _____

"When thou goest forth to war against thine enemies,

and the Lord thy God hath delivered them into thine

hands, and thou hast taken them captive."

Deuteronomy 21:10

Manna:

Today, our primary enemies are not physical. They are spiritual.

Our weapons of choice are not physical objects. They are

spiritual. Our battlefields are not earthly geographical plains.

They are spiritual realms on heavenly plains.

The enemies the Lord delivered us to take captive in war are

not physically flesh and blood. They are renegade spirits of the

devil's army that battle against our minds and existence.

As prisoners of hope, together we will obliterate the armies of

captivity, rebellion, unbelief, bitterness, crime against humanity,

and fears! "For we wrestle not against flesh and blood, but against

principalities, against powers, against the rulers of the darkness

of this world, against spiritual wickedness in high places."

Can you see the need for us to live and walk in the Spirit?

Yes _____

No _____

"Awake, awake, Deborah: awake, awake, utter a song: arise,
Barak, and lead thy captivity captive, thou son of Abinoam."

Judges 5:12

Manna:

Awake thou mighty prisoners of hope. Men and women
alike arise to your cause and your purpose destined by God.
Ignite your fire of hope. "Casting down imagination, and
every high thing that exalteth itself against the knowledge
of God, and bring into captivity every thought to the
obedience of Christ. And having a readiness to revenge
all disobedience when your obedience is fulfilled."

Crush that retarded spirit of unforgiveness,

unbelief, and stubbornness.

"Awake out of sleep: for now is our salvation nearer than
when we believed . . ." "The day is at hand . . ." "Let us put
on the Lord Jesus Christ and make no provision for the flesh,
to fulfill the lusts thereof." We are sons and daughters of
God. Instrument of His praise. Utter your song of praise.

Will you?

Yes _____

No _____

"And so return unto thee with all their heart, and with all
their soul, in the land of their enemies, which led them
away captive, and pray unto thee toward their land, which
thou gavest unto their fathers, the city which thou hast
chosen, and the house which I have built for thy name.
And forgive thy people that have sinned against thee, and all
their transgressions wherein they have transgressed against
thee, and give them compassion before them who carried
them captive, that they may have compassion on them."

1 Kings 8:48, 50

Manna:

From the deepest and darkest dungeons of sin, defeat,
and failure—with a repentant heart, you can turn to God
who will favor you in unspeakable ways, crown you with
compassion, and reward you double for your trouble. Amen!

"When a man's ways please the Lord, he maketh
even his enemies to be at peace with him."

Prisoners of hope, do you see how forgiving and giving God is?

Yes _____

No _____

"And the Syrians had gone out by companies, and
had brought away captives out of the land of Israel a
little maid; and she waited on Naaman's wife."
2 Kings 5:2
Manna:
You may be a young teenage girl confined in a youth Detention
facility, or swept away in the web of sex trafficking, or been
kidnapped for various reasons—enduring mental and physical
torture at the hands of your captors who have taken you captive.
I want you to know God has not forgotten you. You are
the apple of His eye. You will be delivered and set free.
Angels are on their way right now to rescue you.
God sent me with this message just for you. The prisoners
of hope, and the world will not forget you.
Jesus loves you. You have greatness in you.
Believe this, okay?
Yes _____
No _____

"And he answered, Thou shalt not smite them: wouldest
thou smite those whom thou hast taken captive with the
sword and with the bow? Set bread and water before them,
that they may eat and drink, and go to their master?"

2 Kings 6:22

Manna:

The character in heart of the prisoners of hope is to show mercy
even in the face of affliction thereby expressing the heart of our God
who declares, "I will have mercy upon whom I will have mercy."

We choose to have mercy.

Will you?

"He hath shown thee, O man, what is good; and what
doth the Lord require of thee but to do justly, and to
love mercy, and to walk humbly with thy God."

Feed your enemy. It is the door to your miracle.

Pray for them. It is access to your reward.

Will you comply?

Yes _____

No _____

"In the days of Pekah king of Israel came Tiglath-Pileser
king of Assyria, and took Ijon, and Abel-beth-maachah, and
Janoah, and Kedesh, and Hazor, and Gilead, and Galilee, all
the land of Naphtali, and carried them captive to Assyria."

2 Kings 15:29

Manna:

King Satan from the kingdom of fire, and prince of the air, and
ruler of darkness has invaded nations, and taken captive generations,
holding people hostage in unbelief, and genetic make-up.

He secluded and cut off nations of people from the
rest of the world, and with his weapon of mass-
destruction, he daily breathes his threats of terror.

He came to steal, kill, and destroy. But Jesus came that
we might have life, and have it more abundantly.

Prisoners of hope, we are the offspring of God. The
royal blood-line. Partakers of His divine nature.

Will you remember this?

Yes _____

No _____

"And the king of Assyria hearkened unto him: for the king
of Assyria went up against Damascus, and took it, and
carried the people of it captive to Kir, and slew Rezin.
And all the men of might, even seven thousand, and craftsmen
and smiths a thousand, and all that were strong and apt for war,
even them the king of Babylon brought captive to Babylon."

2 Kings 16:9; 24:16

Manna:

Prisoners of hope, let the Word of God captivate you. Be obsessed
with the Word of God until it slew self. Become obsessive in
your relationship with the Holy Spirit until His will is your
only will. The Holy Ghost is perfectly compatible with you.
Only He can navigate you out of this captive imprisonment.
"Turn you at my reproof: behold, I will pour out my spirit
unto you, I will make known my words unto you."

Will you turn to the Lord today?

Yes _____

No _____

"Beerah his son, whom Tilgath-Pileser king of Assyria
carried away captive: he was prince of the Reubenites."

1 Chronicles 5:6

Manna:

You may have been the prize trophy of your family. The son
of pride and joy who glued a union together. The prince
of your family, full of promise and brilliantly beaming the
light of hope—when suddenly carried away captive. All
of your hopes seemed shattered as the judge pronounced
the life sentence against you. But immediately there was
an objection from the Word of God in 1 John 5:9.

"If we receive the witness of men, the witness of God is greater..."

And Heaven said, "Sustained!"

No one's words can out-Christ the Christ.

Prisoners of hope, hope in the Prince of peace Christ
Jesus. He is able to turn the tide of the captive.

"For we are saved by hope: but hope that is seen is not: for
what a man seeth, why doth he yet hope for? But if we hope
for that we see not, then do we with patience wait for it."

Have you put your hope in Jesus for your day of freedom?

Yes _____

No _____

"Yet if they bethink themselves in the land whither
they are carried captive, and turn and pray unto thee
in the land of their captivity, saying, We have sinned,
we have done amiss, and have dealt wickedly."

2 Chronicles 6:37

Manna:

Your present situation requires one thing
to change. You must repent.
Confess your sins and be baptized in the name of Jesus Christ for
the remission of your sins, and you will receive the gift of the Holy
Ghost who instantly will begin the enforcement of your change.
"Therefore if any man be in Christ, he is a new creature: old
things are passed away: behold, all things are become new."
Prisoners of hope, your lives are now governed by the
supernatural plans of God in Christ. Expect the impossible.
You are exposed to an avalanche of uncommon divine change,
because of whose you now are and whom you now serve.

Do you receive this?

Yes _____

No _____

"And other ten thousand left alive did the children of
Judah carry away captive, and brought them unto the
top of the rock, and cast them down from the top of
the rock that they all were broken in pieces."

2 Chronicles 25:12

Manna:

Jesus penetrated this world with the inescapable
unconditional love of God in which He barricaded the
lives of every prisoner of hope under His blood.

No powers that be shall take you captive and cast you down
from the top of any rock and break you in pieces.

The unpredictable wisdom of God is your defense. He
will perform astonishing, extraordinary, and miraculous
works for you like no man has never seen.

"Then I beheld all the work of God, that a man cannot find
out the work that is done under the sun: because though a man
labor to seek it out, yet he shall not find it; yea further; though a
wise man think to know it, yet shall he not be able to find it."

Are you ready to experience the customized life
God has packaged personally for you?

Yes _____

No _____

"And the children of Israel carried away captive of their brethren
two hundred thousand, women, sons, and daughters, and took also
away much spoil from them, and brought the spoil to Samaria.
Now hear me therefore, and deliver the captives
again, which ye have taken captive, of your brethren:
for the fierce wrath of the Lord is upon you."
2 Chronicles 28:8, 11
Manna:
The sovereign God is speaking right now to your
captors' hearts, warning them that Jesus has already
paid the sentence of death for your deliverance.
Now hear this, prisoners of hope. God has spoken on your behalf,
and men do well to obey, and dismantle the chains of captivity.
"By mercy and truth iniquity is purged: and by
the fear of the Lord men depart from evil."
"When a man's ways please the Lord, he maketh
even his enemies to be at peace with him."
Do you know that to please God is rewarding?

Yes _____

No _____

"For if ye turn again unto the Lord, your brethren and your children shall find compassion before them that lead them captive, so that they shall come again into the land: for the Lord your God is gracious and merciful, and will not turn away his face from you, if ye return unto him."

2 Chronicles 30:9

Manna:

Prisoners of hope, some 331 times the Scripture proclaims the sobering declaration "if" as an invitation to warn and awaken men, women, families, and nations to repent of their sins— turn from their wicked ways, and turn to the living God who will abundantly pardon, and send showers of blessings, setting captives free, restoring broken families, and healing nations. "If you be willing and obedient, ye shall eat the good of the land."

See sickness, diseases, and poverty wiped away. Lost loved ones and generations come to Christ.

Would you like to be a part of this experience?

Yes _____

No _____

"Thou hast ascended on high, thou hast led captivity captive:

thou hast received gifts for men; yea, for the rebellious

also, that the Lord God might dwell among them.

For there they that carried us away captive required

of us a song; and they that wasted us required of us

mirth, saying, sing us one of the songs of Zion."

Psalm 78:18; 137:3

Manna:

The gifts Jesus received from God for us prisoners

of hope are showering down today from heaven.

Prison doors must be opened for you.

Go ahead and sing the Lord's song of Zion in this strange

land of your captivity, because the table has been turned

over two thousand years ago by Jesus himself.

You are free.

Do you believe?

Yes _____

No _____

"Then shalt thou say in thine heart, Who hath begotten me
these, seeing I have lost my children, and am desolate, a captive,
and removing to and fro? And who hath brought up these?
Behold, I was left alone; these, where had they been?
Shall the prey be taken from the mighty,
or the lawful captive delivered?
The captive exile hasteneth that he may be loosed, and that
he should not die in the pit, nor that his bread should fail.
Shake thyself from the dust; arise and sit down, O Jerusalem: loose
thyself from the bands of thy neck, O captive daughter of Zion."
Isaiah 49:21, 24; 51:14; 52:2

Manna:
The unprecedented grace of God, and the love of Jesus
Christ by the power of the Holy Ghost is able to set
all lawful prisoners of hope free from captivity.

Do you believe?

Yes _____

No _____

"It came also in the days of Jehoiakim the son of

Judah, unto the end of the eleventh year of Zedekiah

the son of Josiah king of Judah, unto the carrying

away of Jerusalem captive in the fifth month.

But if ye will not hear it, my soul shall weep in secret places

for your pride; and mine eye shall weep sore, and run down

with tears, because the Lord's flock is carried away captive.

The cities of the south shall be shut up, and none

shall open them: Judah shall be carried away captive

all of it, it shall be wholly carried away captive."

Jeremiah 1:3; 13:17, 19

Manna:

Stop! Have you heard of the great reversal of all captives, which

took place at Golgotha? There Jesus hammered the gavel from

his dying cross: It is finished. Prisoners of hope, you are free.

Got it?

Yes _____

No _____

"For thus saith the Lord, Behold, I will make thee a terror
to thyself, and to all thy friends: and they shall fall by the
sword of their enemies, and I will give all Judah into the
hand of the king of Babylon, and he shall carry them captive
into Babylon, and shall slay them with the sword.
But he shall die in the place whither they have led
him captive, and shall see this land no more."

Jeremiah 20:4; 22:12

Manna:

No longer shall you be a terror to yourself, and your friends,
because you are born again, and have the nature of Jesus Christ
beaming through you, the Light of God's love to the world.

This is your freedom unconditionally. Amen!

Agree?

Yes _____

No _____

"The Lord showed me, and behold, two baskets of figs were set
before the temple of the Lord, after that Nebuchadnezzar king of
Babylon had carried away captive Jeconiah the son of Jehoiakim
king of Judah, and the princes of Judah, with the carpenters and
smiths, from Jerusalem, and had brought them to Babylon.
Thus saith the Lord, the God of Israel; Like these good
figs, so will I acknowledge them that are carried away
captive of Judah, whom I have sent out of this place
into the land of the Chaldeans for their good."
Jeremiah 24:1, 5
Manna:
It is amazing how God will not let those who
are carried away captive go unnoticed.
And He turns what seems to be bad into good.
Will you trust Him?
Yes _____
No _____

"Which Nebuchadnezzar king of Babylon took
not, when he carried away captive Jeconiah the son
of Jehoiakim king of Judah and Jerusalem.
Even the prophet Jeremiah said, Amen: the Lord do so:
the Lord perform thy words which thou hast prophesied,
to bring again the vessels of the Lord's house, and all that
is carried away captive, from Babylon into this place."
Jeremiah 27:20; 28:6

Manna:

Your confession can transition your complacency
and confusion from captive chains to the power of
Christ's reign. So, prophesy, prisoners of hope.
You are destined to reign in this life and throughout eternity.
Will you say Amen to this?

Yes _____

No _____

"Now these are the words of the letter that Jeremiah the
prophet sent from Jerusalem unto the residue of the elders
which were carried away captives, and to the priests and to
the prophets and to all the people whom Nebuchadnezzar
had carried away captive from Jerusalem to Babylon.
And I will be found of you saith the Lord: and I will turn
away your captivity, and I will gather you from all the
nations, and from all the places whither I have driven you,
saith the Lord; and I will bring you again into the place
whence I caused you to be carried away captive."
Jeremiah 29:1, 14
Manna:
God's greatest pleasure is to turn around
every prisoner of hope's captivity.
Is this too hard for God to do?
Yes _____
No _____

"Then Nebuzar-adan the captain of the guard carried away captive into Babylon the remnant of the people that remained in the city, and those that fell away, that fell to him, with the rest of the people that remained. The word that came to Jeremiah from the Lord, after that Nebuzar-adan the captain of the guard had let him go from Ramah, when he had taken him being bound in chain among all that were carried away captive of Jerusalem and Judah, which were carried away captive unto Babylon. Now when all the captains of the forces which were in the fields, even they and their men, heard that the king of Babylon had made Gedaliah the son of Ahikam governor in the land, and had committed unto him men, and women, and children, and of the poor of the land, of them that were not carried away captive to Babylon."

Jeremiah 39:9; 40:1, 7

Manna:

Prisoners of hope, the strength of your freedom is your hope. Hope is an engine for miracles.

Agree?

Yes _____

No _____

"Then Ishmael carried away captive all the residue of the people that were in Mizpah, even the king's daughters, and all the people that remained in Mizpah, whom Nebuzar-adan the captain of the guard had committed to Gedaliah the son of Ahikam: and Ishmael the son of Nethaniah carried them away captive, and departed to go over to the Ammonites.

So all the people that Ishmael had carried away captive from Mizpah cast about and returned, and went unto Johanan the son of Kareah."

Jeremiah 41:10, 14

Manna:

I have good news for you today.

Christ Jesus destroyed the captive-carrying scheme of Ishmael and all the others. Dress your mind in hope. Jesus set free the prisoners of hope.

Are you ready to be free indeed?

Yes _____

No _____

"Then Nebuzar-adan the captain of the guard carried away
captive certain of the poor of the people, and the residue of the
people that remained in the city, and those that fell away, that
fell to the king of Babylon, and the rest of the multitude.
And the king of Babylon smote them, and put them
to death in Riblah in the land of Hamath. Thus Judah
was carried away captive out of his own land.
This is the people whom Nebuchadnezzar carried away captive:
in the seventh year three thousand Jews and three and twenty."
Jeremiah 52:15, 27, 28

Manna:

Being poor is not a crime to be carried away captive. A life
without Jesus is the greatest crime against God and self.
Thank God for the grace of Christ who gave up his riches, and
became poor that we, prisoners of hope, might become rich.
Will you give Jesus your poverty for his riches?

Yes _____

No _____

"In the eighteenth year of Nebuchadnezzar he carried away captive from Jerusalem eight hundred thirty and two persons. In the three and twentieth year of Nebuchadnezzar Nebuzar-adan the captain of the guard carried away captive of the Jews seven hundred forty and five persons: all the persons were four thousand and six hundred."

Jeremiah 52:29–30

Manna:

The alarm is calm beyond the norm: to overcome the harm of the storm captive spawn to disarm the prisoners of hope in every form. Captive bars are torn.

Go ahead, raise your arms. Christ is born.

Sealed in heart; the hope of glory.

Is Christ in your heart?

Yes _____

No _____

"Thus saith the Lord; For thee transgression of Gaza, and for four,
I will not turn away the punishment thereof; because they carried
away captive the whole captivity, to deliver them up to Edom.
Therefore now shall they go captive with the first that go captive,
and the banquet of them that stretched themselves shall be removed.
For thus Amos saith, Jeroboam shall die by the sword, and
Israel shall surely be led away captive out of their own land."

Amos 1:6; 6:7; 7:11

Manna:

I have a message for you from God. All your sins were forgiven on
the cross at Calvary.

Jesus paid for your transgression with His blood.

You do not have to live a life of sin any more being
plagued by captivity. You are free, prisoners of hope.

Do you receive this message?

Yes _____

No _____

"In the day that thou stoodest on the other side, in the day that the strangers carried away captive his forces, and foreigners entered into his gates, and cast lots upon Jerusalem, even thou wast as one of them."

Obadiah 11

"And Huzzah shall be led away captive, she shall be brought up, and her maids shall lead her as with the voice of doves, laboring upon their breasts."

Nahum 2:7

Manna:

Consider yourself supremely chosen by God for this season. You are standing on the right side of the cross of Jesus Christ. Heaven's history is written and sealed.

No more shall you be carried away into captivity.

Who the Son set free is free indeed. Amen.

Will you accept this?

Yes _____

No _____

"And they shall fall by the edge of the sword, and shall be led away
captive into all nations: and Jerusalem shall be trodden down
of the Gentiles, until the times of the Gentiles be fulfilled."

St. Luke 21:24

"Wherefore he saith, When he ascended up on high,
he led captivity captive, and gave gifts unto men."

Ephesians 4:8

Manna:

Cancel the mindset that being a captive renders you
powerless. The key to your freedom is your attitude.

Hope is your strength to turn that key.

Jesus took captivity captive on high, and sealed a
gift in you to be released into the world.

He said, "Behold, I set before you an open door."

Can you see it?

Yes _____

No _____

"And that they may recover themselves out of the snare

of the devil, who are taken captive by him at his will.

For of this sort are they which creep into houses, and lead captive

silly women laden with sins, led away with divers lusts."

2 Timothy 2:26; 3:6

Manna:

Fear not the walls and bars surrounding you, prisoners of hope

in captivity. A stone tomb sealed with a mega-ton rock failed

to restrain the lifeless body of Jesus. He triumphed over the

confines of the tomb. How can the devil obstruct your way of

deliverance with the resurrection power of Jesus at work in you?

Know ye not that your body is the temple of the Holy Ghost?

Yes _____

No _____

CHAPTER 6

Captives

"And Laban said to Jacob, What hast thou done, that
thou hast stolen away unawares to me, and carried away
my daughters, as captives taken with the sword?"

Genesis 31:26

Manna:

It was done in public on a hill called the skull. Not in darkness,
but in the light. Jesus took back all the devil had stolen and
carried away as captive, and returned it to the prisoners of
hope. Take back your life. Claim your freedom. Declare that
you are the righteousness of God in Christ. Now act like it.

Will you?

Yes _____

No _____

"And the children of Israel took all the women of Midian captives,

and their cattle, and all their flocks, and all their goods.

And they brought the captives, and the prey, and the

spoil, unto Moses, and Eleazar the priest, and unto the

congregation of the children of Israel, unto the camp at

the plains of Moab, which are by Jordan near Jericho.

And do ye abide without the camp seven days: whosoever

hath killed any person, and whosoever hath touched any slain,

purify both yourselves and your captives on the seventh day."

Numbers 31:9, 12, 19

Manna:

The days referred to above are over and long gone for the prisoners

of hope. God has given us a more abundant life through His grace.

Thank God!

Will you?

Yes _____

No _____

"And seest among the captives a beautiful woman, and hast a
desire unto her, that thou wouldest have her to thy wife.
I will make mine arrows drunk with blood, and my sword shall
devour flesh; and that, with the blood of the slain and of the
captives, from the beginning of revengers upon the enemy."
Deuteronomy 21:11; 32:42

Manna:

Prisoners of hope, men and women tainted by the residue
of various forms of oppressions—Do not lose heart.
The Word of God is your irreversible judgment of
conviction declaring you free by the blood of Jesus. Now
rest in Jesus my dear sisters and brothers. He delivered
the captives, and healed the broken-hearted.

Will you rest in Him?

Yes _____

No _____

"And had taken the women captives, that were
therein: they slew not any, either great or small, but
carried them away, and went on their way.
So David and his men came to the city, and behold,
it was burnt with fire; and their wives, and their sons,
and their daughters, were taken captives."

1 Samuel 30:2–3

Manna:

How grievous were the ruthless acts committed against
the women and children who were led away as captives
in the days of old? Our hearts quake over them, and for
those today who are faced with similar situations.
Prisoners of hope, lift your voice for our captive sisters. Do
not stop praying until every one of them is set free.
Can you agree to pray with me for women in captivity?

Yes _____

No _____

"If they sin against thee, (for there is no man that
sinneth not,) and thou be angry with them, and deliver
them to the enemy, so that they carry them away
captives unto the land of the enemy, far or near;
Yet if they shall bethink themselves in the land whither they were
carried captives, and repent, and make supplication unto thee
in the land of them that carried them captives, saying, We have
sinned, and have done perversely, we have committed wickedness."

1 Kings 8:46–47

Manna:

Prisoners of hope, God loves you.

Your sins are forgiven and forgotten.

God will never be angry with you.

Glory! Alleluia! News flash! Jesus solved your sin problem over
two thousand years ago. Consider yourself favored by God.

He loves you with an everlasting love.

Have you ever thought of that?

Yes _____

No _____

"And he carried away all Jerusalem, and all the princes,
and all the mighty men of valor, even ten thousand
captives, and all the craftsmen and smiths: none remained,
save the poorest sort of the people of the land."

2 Kings 24:14

Manna:

Once upon a time, you were carried away. All of your dreams, all
of your goals, all of your skills, all of your innocence, your youth,
your manhood, your woman-hood. The morals of your upbringing
were carried away by the storms of sin at the hands of the devil.
But Mercy got up off His throne in heaven, and came down in
the person of Jesus Christ, and rescued you with arms of love.
Christ regained your creative power for you prisoners of
hope. You were created and ordained from the womb by
God to be His gifted workers, with uncommon witty ideas
to innovate the world with the everlasting gospel.

You thought you lost your talents, right?

Do you see how great our God is?

Yes _____

No _____

"If they sin against thee, for there is no man which
sinneth not, and thou be angry with them, and deliver
them over before their enemies, and they carry them
away captives unto a land far off or near."

2 Chronicles 6:36

Manna:

Wow! What a treacherous journey.

Sin took me to places I never dreamt I could return from. It
kept me tangled in things longer than I intended to stay. It cost
me way more than I had bargained for. I almost lost my life.
Sin chiseled a hole in my heart, and stole a part of my family.

Brothers and sisters, if you are reading this, open
your heart to Jesus, or else sin will destroy you.

The Bible said, "We all sinned."

Now listen to me! Sin is nothing to toy with. Repent before it
is too late. Open your heart to Jesus right now. Romans 10:9.
Have you repented and do you believe these words right now?

Yes _____

No _____

"Wherefore the Lord his God delivered him into the hand of the king of Syria; and they smote him, and carried away a great multitude of them captives, and brought them to Damascus. And he was also delivered into the hand of the king of Israel, who smote him with a great slaughter.

Now hear me therefore, and deliver the captives again, which ye have taken captive of your brethren: for the fierce wrath of the Lord is upon you."

2 Chronicles 28:5, 11

Manna:

Shackles are broken off; captives wounded and weakened in captivity are ordered free. Rags of desolation are falling off troubled minds. God has spoken, "Awake, awake," Prisoners of hope, your God has rewarded you double for all your trouble.

Did you think God has forgotten you?

Yes _____

No _____

"And said unto them, Ye shall not bring in the captives hither:
for whereas we have offended against the Lord already, ye
intend to add more to our sins and to our trespass: for our
trespass is great, and there is fierce wrath against Israel.
So the armed men left the captives and the spoil
before the princes and all the congregation.
And the men which were expressed by name rose up, and took
the captives, and with the spoil clothed all that were naked
among them, and arrayed them and shod them, and gave them
to eat and drink, and anointed them, and carried them all the
feeble of them upon asses, brought them to Jericho, the city of
palm trees, to their brethren: then they returned to Samaria.
For again the Edomites had come and smitten
Judah, and carried away captives."
2 Chronicles 28:13–15, 17
Manna:
When the uncommon favor of God rests upon you, prisoners
of hope, even your captors hasten your deliverance.
Are you ready?
Yes _____
No _____

"He made them also to be pitied of all
those that carried them captives."
Psalm 104:46

Manna:

God is able to condition the hearts of those who took
you captive with compassion. He will cause them to do
you good. Never underestimate how much you are loved
by God. Be of high expectation, prisoners of hope.
Goodness and mercy are following you.

Are your expectations high?

Yes _____

No _____

"And the people shall take them, and bring them to their place:
and the house of Israel shall possess them in the land of the Lord
for servants and handmaids: and they shall take them captives,
whose captives they were; and they shall rule over their oppressors.
So shall the king of Assyria lead away the Egyptians prisoners,
and the Ethiopians captives, young and old, naked and barefoot,
even with their buttocks uncovered, to the shame of Egypt.
I have raised him up in righteousness, and I will direct all his
ways: he shall build my city, and he shall let go my captives,
not for price nor reward, saith the Lord of hosts."

Isaiah 14:2; 20:4; 45:13

Manna:

I dare you to believe God to His Word, you prisoners of hope.
Throw your life completely in His hand, and watch
Him unravel you out of your captor's hands.

Will you trust Him?

Yes _____

No _____

"But thus saith the Lord, Even the captives of the
mighty shall be taken away, and the prey of the terrible
shall be delivered: for I will contend with him that
contendeth with thee, and I will save thy children.
The Spirit of the Lord God is upon me, because the Lord hath
anointed me to preach good tidings unto the meek; he hath sent
me to bind up the broken-hearted, to proclaim liberty to the
captives, and the opening of the prison to them that are bound."

Isaiah 49:25; 61:1

Manna:

Prisoners of hope, whosoever toucheth you toucheth the apple
of God's eye. God will fight tooth and nail for you against them
that carried you away captives. He will save your children too.
That is why He sent His only begotten Son from heaven to
the cradle; from the cradle to the cross; from the cross to the
grave; and from the grave to the pits of hell. Jesus beat that old
devil, and took the keys of hell and death to redeem you.

Agree?

Yes _____

No _____

"And I will bring again to this place Jeconiah the son
of Jehoiakim king of Judah, with all the captives of
Judah, that went into Babylon, saith the Lord: for
I will break the yoke of the king of Babylon.
Now these are the words of the letter that Jeremiah the
prophet sent from Jerusalem unto the residue of the elders
which were carried away captives, and to the priests, and to
the prophets, and to all the people whom Nebuchadnezzar
had carried away captive from Jerusalem to Babylon.
Thus saith the Lord of hosts, the God of Israel, unto
all that are carried away captives, whom I have caused
to be carried away from Jerusalem unto Babylon.
And seek the peace of the city whither I have caused
you to be carried away captives, and pray unto the Lord
for it: for in the peace thereof shall ye have peace."
Jeremiah 28:4; 29:1, 4, 7

Manna:

Obey God's Word, and pray for peace in the place
you are at. Prayer is a world-changing tool.

Agree?

Yes _____

No _____

"But Baruch the son of Neriah setteth thee against us, for to
deliver us, into the hand of the Chaldeans, that they might
put us to death, and carry us away captives into Babylon.
And I will kindle a fire in the houses of the gods of Egypt; and
he shall burn them, and carry them away captives: and he shall
array himself with the land of Egypt, as a shepherd putteth on
his garment; and he shall go forth from thence in peace."

Jeremiah 43:3, 12

Manna:

The only plan that can succeed against your life and future
today is Jeremiah 29:11. Shout hallelujah! Praise the Lord!

Prisoners of hope, our God is a consuming fire.

And you are filled with Holy Ghost fire.

Like Father, like son, you are a consuming fire.

So let your Christian fire shine Christ's love

in the place where you reside.

Will you do that for Jesus?

Yes _____

No _____

"Woe be unto thee, O Moab! the people of Chemosh perisheth:
for thy sons are taken captives, and thy daughters captives.
Thus saith the Lord of hosts; The children of Israel and the
children of Judah were oppressed together: and all that took
them captives held them fast; they refuse to let them go."

Jeremiah 48:46; 50:33

Manna:

Once you receive Jesus the Christ as your personal Savior, and
Lord over your life. Prisoners of hope, you are unstoppable.
If Pharaoh could not hold the beloved children of Israel in Egypt,
and the grave could not hold the lifeless body of Jesus. Who or
what on earth can hold back the prisoners of hope from victory?

You are unstoppable!

Do you believe?

Yes _____

No _____

"Now it came to pass in the thirtieth year, in the fourth month, in the fifth day of the month, as I was among the captives by the river of Chebar, that the heavens were opened, and I saw visions of God.
And they that escape of you shall remember me among the nations whither they shall be carried captives, because I am broken with their whorish heart, which hath departed from me, and with their eyes, which go a whoring after their idols: and they shall loathe themselves for the evils which they have committed in all their abominations.
When I shall bring again their captivity, the captivity of Sodom and her daughters, the captivity of Samaria and her daughters, then will I bring again the captivity of thy captives in the midst of them."
Ezekiel 1:1; 6:9; 16:53

Manna:

God's heart is open wider than the heavens for you. Cleave unto Him with an obsession, and do not forget His goodness and love.

Will you?

Yes _____

No _____

"Then Arioch brought in Daniel before the king in haste, and
said thus unto him, I have found a man of the captives of Judah,
that will make known unto the king the interpretation.
And shall also carry captives into Egypt their gods, with their
princes, and with their precious vessels of silver and of gold;
and he shall continue more years than the king of the north."

Daniel 2:25; 11:8

Manna:

Prisoners of hope, you carry the aroma of the anointed Christ on
you. You are the beacon of hope to those around you, including
the captors who carried you away. You are the bearer of precious
cargo. Holy Ghost filled. Like brother Daniel, you can become a
magnet and a solution in the band of God's men, sought after by
men in their times of trouble. Your gift will bring you before kings.

You are not just human. One-third of you is
straight-up wall-to-wall Holy Ghost spread.

The new creature rarity.

Are you seeing what God sees in you?

Yes _____

No _____

"The Spirit of the Lord is upon me, because he hath anointed me to preach the gospel to the poor; he hath sent me to heal the broken-hearted, to preach deliverance to the captives, and recovering of sight to the blind, to set at liberty them that are bruised."

Luke 4:18

Manna:

Jesus came to this world on a mission to make every prisoner of hope whole, and He left no stone unturned.

He preached the gospel, healed the brokenhearted, instructed deliverance to the captives, restored sight to the blind, and freed those bruised.

Are you suffering a bruised spirit because of a family or friend on top of being in captivity?

Receive the Lord's healing and forgive.

Will you?

Yes _____

No _____

CHAPTER 7

Captivity

"Woe to thee, Moab! thou art undone, O people of Chemosh:
he hath given his sons that escaped, and his daughters
into captivity unto Sihon king of the Amorites."

Numbers 21:29

Manna:

Prisoners of hope, you may be one who can testify about the
betrayal by a spouse, parents, loved ones, or friends, who have
given you over to those who hold you in captivity today.

Nevertheless, your faith in Jesus has given you the
strength and grace to forgive. And you have seized upon
the sure promise of God's Word for comfort!

As it is written: "When my father and my mother forsake
me, then the Lord will take me up" (Ps. 27:10).

Are you glad God has not forgotten you?

Yes _____

No _____

"And she shall put the raiment of her captivity from off her,
and shall remain in thine house, and bewail her father and
her mother a full month: and after that thou shalt go in
unto her, and be her husband, and she shall be thy wife.
Thou shalt beget sons and daughters, but thou shalt
not enjoy them; for they shall go into captivity.
That then the Lord thy God will turn thy captivity, and have
compassion upon thee, and will return and gather thee from all
the nations whither the Lord thy God hath scattered thee."

Deuteronomy 21:13; 28:14; 30:3

Manna:

God has given us all things to enjoy, and wherever captivity seems
to stand in the way, He magnifies His mercy to sustain His Word.

No wife, or woman, shall be taken by force.

The curse is broken and sons and daughters
will be enjoyed captivity-free.

It is over! Receive His mercy and compassion.

Will you?

Yes _____

No _____

"Awake, awake, Deborah: awake, awake, utter a song: arise,

Barak, and lead thy captivity captive, thou son of Abinoam.

And the children of Dan set up the graven image: and Jonathan,

the son of Gershom, the son of Manasseh, he and his sons were

priests to the tribe of Dan until the day of the captivity of the land."

Judges 5:12; 18:30

Manna:

Listen up! We are no longer sleepers. We are prisoners of hope.

People of purpose are uniquely called upon by God. They are

destined to reign by the power of the Lord Jesus Christ, and

enriched by the unmatchable Holy Spirit. Prisoners of hope, rouse

the lost and sleeping sinners into the Light and Life of Jesus.

Awaken to hope, your day of uncommon deliverance is at hand.

Soon your captivity will be no more. God has a miracle for you.

Will you receive it?

Yes _____

No _____

"And he carried away Jehoiakim to Babylon, and the king's mother, and the king's wives, and his officers, and the mighty of the land, those carried he into captivity from Jerusalem to Babylon.
And it came to pass in the seven and thirtieth year of the captivity of Jehoiakim king of Judah, in the twelfth month, on the seven and twentieth day of the month, that Evil-merodach king of Babylon, in the year that he began to reign, did lift up the head of Jehoiakim king of Judah out of prison."

2 Kings 24:15; 25:27

Manna:

The Holy Scriptures have made the prisoners
of hope wise unto salvation.
The vision is clear. The responsibility is in
your hand for your children's future.
The cycle of captivity must end where you stand. The
curse is over at the cross. You must take home this new life
Jesus has given to you, your children and your family.

Will you?

Yes _____

No _____

"For there fell down many slain, because the war was of

God. And they dwelt in their steads until the captivity.

And Jehozadak went into captivity, when the Lord carried

away Judah and Jerusalem by the hand of Nebuchadnezzar."

1 Chronicles 5:22; 6:15

Manna:

In Exodus we read, "God is a man of war."

Prisoners of hope, the battle you are up against called captivity is

not yours. "It is the Lord's." Your physical strength cannot fight this

enemy.

However, he can be defeated, but "not by might nor

by power, but by My Spirit, saith the Lord."

Now can you be of good courage, and wait

upon the Lord for your victory?

Yes _____

No _____

"Yet if they bethink themselves in the land whither
they are carried captive, and turn and pray unto thee
in the land of their captivity, saying, We have sinned,
we have done amiss, and have dealt wickedly:
If they return to thee with all their heart and with all their soul
in the land of their captivity, whither they have carried them
captives, and pray toward their land, which thou gavest unto
their fathers, and toward the city which thou hast chosen,
and toward the house which I have built for thy name.
For lo, our fathers have fallen by the sword, and our sons
and our daughters and our wives are in captivity for this."

2 Chronicles 6:37–38; 29:9

Manna:

The prayer of repentance from the depths of captivity will
consummate the prisoner of hope's plight within God's heart.
A renewed relationship springs forth with unlimited benefits,
and total restoration of all the enemy had stolen.

Have you repented?

Yes _____

No _____

"All the vessels of gold, and of silver were five thousand and four hundred. All these did Sheshbazzar bring up with them of the captivity that were brought up from Babylon unto Jerusalem.

Now these are the children of the province that went up out of the captivity, of those which had been carried away, whom Nebuchadnezzar the king of Babylon had carried away unto Babylon, and came again unto Jerusalem and Judah, every one unto his city.

Now in the second year of their coming unto the house of God at Jerusalem, in the second month, began Zerubbabel the son of Shealtiel, and Jeshua the son of Jozadak, and the remnant of their brethren the priests and the Levites, and all they that were come out of the captivity unto Jerusalem; and appointed the Levites from twenty years old and upward, to set forward the word of the house of the Lord."

Ezra 1:11; 2:1; 3:8

Manna:

Captivity is the seed for obedience to change.

Agree?

Yes _____

No _____

"Now when the adversaries of Judah and Benjamin
heard that the children of the captivity builded
the temple unto the Lord God of Israel.
And the children of Israel, the priests, and the Levites,
and the rest of the children of the captivity, kept
the dedication of this house of God with joy.
And the children of the captivity kept the Passover
upon the fourteenth day of the first month.
For the priests and the Levites were purified together, all of them
were pure, and killed the Passover for all the children of the
captivity, and for their brethren the priests and for themselves."
Ezra 4:1; 6:16, 19, 20

Manna:

For the prisoners of hope, captivity is the place where hidden
dreams, gifts, and talents are discovered and come alive. What
the adversaries meant for bad, you can turn into good.
Prisoners of hope, learn obedience through the things they
suffered. They are following in the footsteps of their Savior.

Are you a dreamer?

Yes _____

No _____

"Also the children of those that had been carried away, which
were come out of the captivity, offered burnt offerings unto
the God of Israel, twelve bullocks for all Israel, ninety and
six rams, seventy and seven lambs, twelve he goats for a sin
offering: all this was a burnt offering unto the Lord.
Since the days of our fathers have we been in a great
trespass unto this day; and for our iniquities have we,
our kings, and our priests, been delivered into the hand
of the kings of the lands, to the sword, to captivity, and
to a spoil, and to confusion of face, as it is this day."

Ezra 8:35; 9:7

Manna:

Know this with assurance, prisoners of hope:
Without Jesus Christ, governing your life sin will eat away at you
one generation at a time. It will pick you apart with captivity,
family oppression, and confusions until you pine away.

"The wages of sin is death; but the gift of God is
eternal life through Jesus Christ our Lord."

Will you receive God's gift Christ Jesus today?

Yes _____

No _____

"And they made proclamation throughout Judah and
Jerusalem unto all the children of the captivity, that they
should gather themselves together unto Jerusalem.
And the children of the captivity did so. And Ezra the priest,
with certain chiefs of the fathers, after the house of their fathers,
and all of them by their names, were separated, and sat down
in the first day of the tenth month to examine the matter."

Ezra 10:7, 16

Manna:

Let this proclamation be heard throughout the world in every
place of captivity. The hour has come for every prisoner of hope to
believe in Jesus, and begin worshiping God in spirit and in truth.

Congregate together with the gospel in your hands.

If that is not your plan, then consider yourself wrong, because
it is the only thing that can truly make you strong.

Do you know there is an eternal land?

If so, do you have a plan?

Yes _____

No _____

"That Hanani, one of my brethren, came, he and certain men of Judah; and I asked them concerning the Jews that had escaped, which were left of the captivity, and concerning Jerusalem. And they said unto me, the remnant that are left of the captivity there in the province are in great affliction and reproach: the wall of Jerusalem also is broken down, and the gates thereof are burnt with fire."

Nehemiah 1:2–3

Manna:

The deck is stacked against you, the judge's decree written and declared, the Haman's of your soul prepared for destruction. Like Esther, the Lord may have you here in captivity "for such a time as this." The plan of Haman did not succeed against our beloved Jewish brothers and sisters, and it surely will not succeed against the prisoners of hope who seek the face of Jesus for those in captivity around the world.

Holy Spirit, inspire us to intercede for the salvation of those who do not know Jesus.

Are you praying?

Yes _____

No _____

"Hear, O our God; for we are despised: and turn
their reproach upon their own head, and give
them for a prey in the land of captivity.
These are the children of the province, that went up out of
the captivity, of those that had been carried away, whom
Nebuchadnezzar the king of Babylon had carried away, and
came again to Jerusalem and Judah, every one unto his city.
And all the congregation of them that were come again out of
the captivity made booths, and sat under the booths: for since
the days of Jeshua the son of Nun unto that day had not the
children of Israel done so. And there was very great gladness."
Nehemiah 4:4; 7:6; 8:17
Manna:
Are you feeling helpless? Then pray!
Despised and cast down? Pray!
Frightened by reproach? Pray!
Rejected and alone? Pray!
The closer prayer gets you to God, the more
you want to stay close to Him.
Prisoners of hope, ". . . draw near to God,
and God will draw near to you."
Have you ever sat in God's presence just praying?
Yes _____
No _____

"Who had been carried away from Jerusalem with the captivity
which had been carried away with Jeconiah king of Judah, whom
Nebuchadnezzar the king of Babylon had carried away."

Esther 2:6

Manna:

Did you ever hear this saying? The world's definition of
insanity is doing the same thing over and over and expecting
different results. Well, for the prisoners of hope, the definition
of sanity is to keep doing the same thing God says to do over
and over regardless of the outcome. "Pray without ceasing."
Keep believing. That is faith on active duty in action. Be like
Abraham. "He staggered not at the promise of God through
unbelief; but was strong in faith, giving glory to God."
Captivity is insanity. Keep standing on God's Word. It will
not fail you, although it may tarry for a while or even years.

Keep believing.

You are not insane. "It is impossible for God to lie."

Is there anything that is too hard for God?

Yes _____

No _____

"And the Lord turned the captivity of Job, when he prepared for his friends: also the Lord gave Job twice as much as he had before."

Job 42:10

Manna:

Who could have known that disaster, destruction of property, loss of family, ill health, and prestige are all forms of captivity? Just ask brother Job. The greatest ambassadors of God all walked the "perp" catwalk of captivity. Brother John the Baptist is counted as the greatest man born of women, saith Jesus. Yet captivity was his doorway into glory. Jesus Himself became the world's most famous human to ever walk the earthly catwalks of captivity. Innocent and without fault, He bore the cross of suffering and shame. Captivity is the enemy of our souls, prisoners of hope. It is written: "The Lord looseth the prisoners." Take note: intercessory prayer is a turning point from captivity. Do you know God wants to give you double for your trouble?

Yes _____

No _____

"Oh that the salvation of Israel were come out of Zion!
When the Lord bringeth back the captivity of his
people, Jacob shall rejoice, and Israel shall be glad.
Thou hast ascended on high, thou hast led captivity captive:
thou hast received gifts for men; yea, for the rebellious
also, that the Lord God might dwell among them.
And delivered his strength into captivity, and
his glory into the enemy's hands.
Lord, thou hast been favorable unto thy land: thou
hast brought back the captivity of Jacob."
Psalm 14:7; 68:18; 78:61; 85:1
Manna:
God supremely rules in all our situations.
He abides among us in all our journeys of captivity.
He is in touch with the very feeling of our
infirmities. Our deliverance is in His hands.
Prisoners of hope, He is our salvation, and He
remains favorable to us. Amen saints.
Agree?
Yes _____
No _____

"When the Lord turned again the captivity of
Zion, we were like them that dream.
Turn again our captivity, O Lord, as the streams in the south."
Psalm 126:1, 4
Manna:

Your freedom from captivity is a good thing. And God said, "No good thing will he withhold from them that walk uprightly." Prisoners of hope, the grace of God in His Son Jesus Christ has burned through all the years of your captivity, and trailing behind is an earthquake of joy and gladness at the news of your return.

Break forth in laughter and singing, prisoners of hope.

You went in weeping, but you will return rejoicing.

Will somebody shout Hallelujah?

Yes _____

No _____

"Therefore my people are gone into captivity, because
they have no knowledge: and their honorable men
famished, and their multitude dried up with thirst.
Behold, the Lord will carry thee away with a
mighty captivity, and will surely cover thee.
They stoop, they bow down together; they could not deliver
the burden, but themselves are gone into captivity."
Isaiah 5:13; 22:17; 46:2

Manna:

From the "thou shall not eat of the tree of knowledge of good
and evil" in Genesis; to the instruction in 2 Peter to "grow
in grace, and in the knowledge of our Lord and Savior Jesus
Christ;" the Bible appeals to the people of God to adhere to
the instruction of "knowledge" 172 times in thirty-five of
its sixty-six books, in one way or another for their good.
Prisoners of hope, the saving knowledge of God in Christ Jesus is
your only preventative life-line to avoid captivity of every form.
Open the Word of God, and build your life
on the knowledge of Jesus Christ.

Will you?

Yes _____

No _____

"And it shall come to pass, if they say unto thee, Whither shall we go forth? then thou shalt tell them, Thus saith the Lord, Such as are for death, to death; and such as are for the sword, to the sword; and such as are for the famine, to the famine; and such as are for the captivity, to the captivity. And then, Pashur, and all that dwell in thine house shall go into captivity: and thou shalt come to Babylon, and there thou shalt die, and shalt be buried there, thou, and all thy friends, to whom thou hast prophesied lies. The wind shall eat up all thy pastors, and thy lovers shall go into captivity: surely then shalt thou be ashamed and confounded for all the wickedness."

Jeremiah 15:2; 20:6; 22:22

Manna:

Prisoners of hope, from here you have one way to go forth—and one way only. That way is into "life and life more abundantly," courtesy of your Savior and Lord Jesus Christ. This cannot be changed.

Did you know that?

Yes _____

No _____

"And I will be found of you, saith the Lord: and I will
turn away your captivity, and will gather you from all the
nations, and from all the places whither I have driven
you, saith the Lord; and I will bring you again into the
place whence I caused you to be carried away captive.
Know that thus saith the Lord of the king that sitteth upon the
throne of David, and of all the people that dwelleth in this city, and
of your brethren that are not gone forth with you into captive."

Jeremiah 29:14, 16

Manna:

Here is where you can find some of God's too-good-to-be-
true promises. Are you listening to God right now?
Prisoners of hope, Jesus has exposed you to God's unlimited
grace. It is falling off heaven's assembly line into your life daily.
Let this sink down into your spirit. Meditate upon
it. Speak it, because God promised it. Amen. He
said, "I will turn away your captivity."
Is this too hard for God to do?

Yes _____

No _____

"Hear ye therefore the word of the Lord, all ye of the
captivity, whom I have sent from Jerusalem to Babylon.
And of them shall be taken up a curse by all the captivity of Judah
which are in Babylon, saying, the Lord make thee like Zedekiah
and like Ahab, whom the king of Babylon roasted in the fire.
For therefore he sent unto us in Babylon, saying, this
captivity is long: build ye houses, and dwell in them;
and plant gardens, and eat the fruit of them.
Send to all them of the captivity, saying, thus saith the
Lord concerning Shemaiah the Nehelamite; Because
that Shemaih hath prophesied unto you, and I sent
him not, and he caused you to trust in a lie."
Jeremiah 29:20, 22, 28, 31
Manna:
Here is the truth! Under the new and eternal covenant of
God in Christ Jesus, we are sent into the world to preach the
gospel, not into captivity to pine away. "And you shall know
the truth, and the truth shall make you free," saith Jesus.
Do you know the truth?
Yes _____
No _____

"For lo, the days come, saith the Lord, that I will bring
again the captivity of my people Israel and Judah, saith
the Lord: and I will cause them to return to the land
that I gave to their fathers, and they shall possess it.
Therefore, fear thou not, O my servant Jacob, saith the Lord;
neither be dismayed, O Israel, for lo, I will save thee from afar, and
thy seed from the land of their captivity; and Jacob shall return,
and shall be in rest, and be quiet, and none shall make him afraid."

Jeremiah 30:3, 10

Manna:

Could this be the day your turn-around finally comes?
Time and time again, God has affirmed that He
will set free His people taken into captivity.
Prisoners of hope, Christ's shed blood on Calvary
qualifies you as recipients of this promise.
So again, I ask: Could this be the day your
turn-around finally comes?

Yes _____

No _____

"Thus saith the Lord of hosts, the God of Israel; As yet they shall use this speech in the land of Judah and in the cities thereof, when I shall bring again their captivity; The Lord bless thee, O habitation of justice, and mountain of holiness.

Men shall by fields for money, and subscribe evidence, and seal them, and take witnesses in the land of Benjamin, and in the place about Jerusalem, and in the cities of Judah, and in the cities of the mountains, and in the cities of the valley, and in the cities of the south: for I will cause their captivity to return, saith the Lord."

Jeremiah 31:23; 32:44

Manna:

Can you see yourself prospering in the future?

The Lord God has given you all the assurances of His Son's creative power in His Word. There is no limitations to your accomplishments and successes in Jesus Christ to the world. Enhance your expectations, prisoners of hope.

Captivity is not your home.

Are you seeing yourself the way God sees you?

Yes _____

No _____

"And I will cause the captivity of Judah and the captivity
of Israel to return, and will build them, as at the first.
The voice of joy, and the voice of gladness, the voice of the
bridegroom, and the voice of the bride, the voice of them that
shall say, Praise the Lord of hosts: for the Lord is good: for
his mercy endureth forever: and of them that shall bring the
sacrifice of praise into the house of the Lord, For I will cause to
return the captivity of the land as at the first, saith the Lord."
Jeremiah 33:7, 11

Manna:

Jesus Christ was, and is, and will always be a builder. He set
captives free from a clogged life of sin in captivity, and then,
He built them anew from the ground up into a holy life of
freedom, joy, and gladness in the Holy Ghost, unto a productive
Christ-centered Christian loving life. Shout Him praise!

Will you live and walk in the Spirit of joy?

Yes _____

No _____

"O thou daughter dwelling in Egypt, furnish

thyself to go into captivity, for Noph shall be

waste and desolate without an inhabitant.

But fear not thou, O my servant Jacob, and be not dismayed,

O Israel: for behold, I will save thee from afar off, and thy

seed from the land of their captivity; and Jacob shall return,

and be in rest and at ease, and none shall make him afraid."

Jeremiah 46:19, 27

Manna:

Once God speaks, His Word stands firm.

The order was given before the foundation of the world.

Jesus would storm the gates of captivity head on for every

son and daughter of God, and superimpose His authority

over captivity, furnishing their lives with the power of

His Spirit to bring the gospel of salvation to those afar

off. And so He said, "My covenant will I not break, nor

alter the thing that is gone out of my lips." Amen!

Are you listening to Jesus?

Yes _____

No _____

"For because thou hast trusted in thy works and in thy
treasures, thou shalt also be taken: and Chemosh shall go forth
into captivity with his priests and his princes together.
Moab hath been at ease from his youth, and he hath
settled on his lees, and hath not been emptied from vessel
to vessel, neither hath he gone into captivity: therefore his
taste remained in him, and his scent is not changed.
Yet will I bring again the captivity of Moab
in the latter days, saith the Lord.
Thus far is the judgment of Moab."
Jeremiah 48:7, 11, 47
Manna:
Prisoners of hope, from the moment you receive Jesus Christ into
your heart, the rite of passage from captivity is open to you.
"Jesus is the way . . ." while ". . . the joy of the Lord is your
strength." Your conversion brings the voices of joy and gladness all
the way to the halls of heaven. Angels rejoice. God will perform all
of His "I will" vows that He makes to you.
Amen!
Do you realize that God has His focus on you?
Yes _____
No _____

"Howl, O Heshbon, for Ai is spoiled: cry, ye daughters

of Rabbah, gird ye with sackcloth; lament, and run

to and fro by the hedges; for their king shall go into

captivity, and his priests and his princes together.

And afterward I will bring again the captivity of

the children of Ammon, saith the Lord.

But it shall come to pass in the latter days, that I will

bring again the captivity of Elam, saith the Lord."

Jeremiah 49:3, 6, 39

Manna:

Jesus is our King of kings, who reigns over your captivity and

takes it captive with a powerful and commanding blow.

The weapon of captivity may form against the prisoners of hope,

but by no means will it prosper. Rejoice O daughters of Jehovah.

Your King is untouchable sitting on the right hand of God's

throne. Publish this in the ears of all people near and far. Amen!

Do you know we are living under the dispensation of grace?

Yes _____

No _____

"And it came to pass in the seven and thirtieth year of the captivity of Jehoiachin king of Judah, in the twelfth month, in the five and twentieth day of the month, that Evil-merodach king of Babylon in the first year of his reign lifted up the head of Jehoiachin king of Judah, and brought him forth out of prison."

Jeremiah 52:31

Manna:

Jesus Christ possesses all power and authority as King of kings over captivity to set the prisoners of hope free. He loved us so much that He washed us from our sins in His own blood, and then presented us as kings and ministers of the gospel unto God Almighty.

That is the style of our Savior on this side of the cross.

Do you recognize the greatness of God on your life?

Yes _____

No _____

"Judah is gone into captivity because of affliction, and because
of great servitude: she dwelleth among the heathen, she findeth
no rest: all her persecutors overtook her between the straits.

Her adversaries are the chief, her enemies prosper; for the
Lord hath afflicted her for the multitude of her transgressions:
her children are gone into captivity before the enemy.

The Lord is righteous; for I have rebelled against his
commandment: hear; I pray you, all people, and behold my
sorrow: my virgins and my young men are gone into captivity."

Lamentation 1:3, 5, 18

Manna:

There is no other resolution for your solution apart
from Jesus. He litigated your case with His life on the
cross of Calvary against the world's greatest leading
prosecutors, and He won. Satan and his demons lost.

The prosperity of the adversaries is short lived.

Your repentance of a broken and contrite heart
has touched God's heart. You are free.

Agree?

Yes _____

No _____

"The prophets have seen vain and foolish things for thee:
and they have not discovered thine iniquity; but have
seen for thee false burdens and causes of banishment.
The punishment of thine iniquity is accomplished, O daughter of
Zion; he will no more carry thee away into captivity: he will visit
thine iniquity, O daughter of Edom; he will discover thy sin."
Lamentation 2:14; 4:22

Manna:

No longer will women be gullible seeking the advice of foolish
whoevers. Your Truth has come. Over 2,000 years ago en route
to the grave, Jesus spoke these words while nailed to the cross
between two thieves. ". . . Jesus knowing that all things were
now accomplished, that the scriptures might be fulfilled, saith,
I thirst." Prisoners of hope, your punishment for sure has
been long accomplished for sin. Pack the bags of your mind
and heart with faith, hope and love. You are going home.
Do you thirst for the Lord Jesus?

Yes _____

No _____

"In the fifth day of the month, which was the

fifth year of king Jehoiachin's captivity.

And go, get thee to them of the captivity, unto the children of

thy people, and speak unto them, and tell them, Thus saith the

Lord God; whether they will hear, or whether they will forbear.

Then I came to them of the captivity at Tel Abib, that

dwelt by the river of Chebar, and I sat where they sat, and

remained there astonished among them seven days."

Ezekiel 1:2; 3:11, 15

Manna:

Real talk! Prisoners of hope, a message is sent to you from God

today. Get to the chapel. Get to the Bible Study with ears, mind,

and heart attentive, in the ready, to hear what "Thus saith the Lord"

to you. Honor the messengers, missionaries and volunteers, "As it is

written, How beautiful are the feet of them that preach the gospel

of peace, and bring glad tidings of good things!" Real talk! Alleluia!

Are you ready to receive your assignment?

Yes _____

No _____

"Afterwards the spirit took me up, and brought me in
vision by the Spirit of God into Chaldea, to them of the
captivity. So the vision that I had seen went up from me.
Then I spake unto them of the captivity all the
things that the Lord had shewed me."

Ezekiel 11:24, 25

Manna:

Here is an amazing thing about God that fascinates the prisoners
of hope. In the deepest, darkest dungeon of solitary confinement
in captivity, where the mind is slowly losing touch with reality,
God, in His sovereignty, breaks through the barriers of sin and
mental instability to reach the hopeless, faithless, and lost sinners,
and embodies them with the resurrection power of Jesus Christ,
to see visions of glory in the Spirit, and the holy Word of Jah.

Thus, the hopeless and faithless become prisoners of hope
built on the revelational knowledge of Jesus Christ in grace.
God said, "Where there is no vision, the people perish . . ."

Proverbs 29:18

Will you agree?

Yes _____

No _____

"Then shalt thou bring forth thy stuff by day in their sight, as stuff for removing: and thou shalt go forth at even in their sight, as they that go forth into captivity. And I did so as I was commanded: I brought forth my stuff by day, as stuff for captivity, and in the evening I digged through the wall with mine hand; I brought it forth in the twilight, and I bare it upon my shoulder in their sight. Say, I am your sign: like as I have done, so shall it be done unto them: they shall remove and go into captivity."

Ezekiel 12:4, 7, 11

Manna:

The greatest demonstration and sign from God this world has ever seen, and will ever experience, is the majestic, historic, world-changing, crowning event of Jesus Christ's resurrection from the dead to life eternal. Time stopped and began as the rock was rolled away from the tomb for the world to view—the *rock* of our salvation who frees us from captivity, and contains all the good stuff we need.

Is He all you need?

Yes _____

No _____

"When I shall bring again their captivity, the captivity
of Sodom and her daughters, and the captivity of
Samaria and her daughters, then will I bring again the
captivity of the captives in the midst of them.
And say unto the Ammonites, Hear the word of the Lord
God; Thus saith the Lord God; Because thou saidst, Aha,
against my sanctuary, when it was profaned, and against
the land of Israel, when it was desolate; and against the
house of Judah, when they went into captivity."

Ezekiel 16:53; 25:3

Manna:

Shout hallelujah, daughters in captivity, favored of God and
loved. He shall bring you out in due time, and exalt you above
all those who reproach you with His incredible kindness. Rest in
the comfort of Jesus' love for you. God takes your case personally,
interceding against all those who say "aha" at your fall.

Do you know how much God delights in you?

Yes _____

No _____

"And I will bring again the captivity of Egypt, and will cause them to return into the land of Pathros, into the land of their habitation; and they shall be there a base kingdom."

Ezekiel 29:14

Manna:

Look deep down into your heart, prisoners of hope, and see God doing the things He promised to do. Spread the wings of your faith, and soar high in confidence of your hope. There is power in your faith to move mountains. Do not second guess the commitment of God's Word to bring you out of captivity. Allow His Word to bring you out of captivity of fears, doubt, shame, addictions to the flesh, anger, bitterness, self-pity, hate, unbelief, drug use, gangs, and every other form of captivity. God offers you total freedom from captivities in Jesus Christ His Son.

Will you accept?

Yes _____

No _____

"The young men of Aven and of Phi-beseth shall fall by
the sword: and these cities shall go into captivity.
At Tehaphnehes also the day shall be darkened, when I
shall break there the yokes of Egypt: and the pomp of
her strength shall cease in her: as for her, a cloud shall
cover her, and her daughters shall go into captivity.
And it came to pass in the twelfth year of our captivity, in the tenth
month, in the fifth day of the month, that one that had escaped
out of Jerusalem came unto me, saying, The city is smitten."

Ezekiel 30:17, 18; 33:21

Manna:

Captivity pains. Captivity mentally drains. Captivity strains,
and deranges. Captivity segregates and humiliates. It separates.
If one escapes the high gates of captivity, there is sure to
be a trail of the lingering story told. Thank God, for the
coming of Christ with the glorious light that encompasses
Him, and the gospel to reconcile, that can never stale.

Can you see with Jesus there is much to gain?

Yes _____

No _____

"And the heathen shall know that the house of Israel went into captivity for their iniquity: because they trespassed against me, therefore hid I my face from them, and gave them into the hand of their enemies: so fell they all by the sword. Therefore thus saith the Lord God, Now will I bring again the captivity of Jacob, and have mercy upon the whole house of Israel, and will be jealous for my holy name. Then shall they know that I am the Lord their God which caused them to be led into captivity among the heathen: but I have gathered them unto their own land, and have left none of them anymore there."

Ezekiel 39:23, 25, 28

Manna:

When the face of Jesus Christ rises like the sun upon you in captivity, open your heart with sincerity and truth to obey the instructions of His Word.

God is jealous, and He comes for His own.

Are you ready to go?

Yes _____

No _____

"In the five and twentieth year of our captivity, in the beginning
of the year, in the tenth day of the month, in the fourteenth
year after that the city was smitten, in the selfsame day the
hand of the Lord was upon me, and brought me thither."

Ezekiel 41:1

Manna:

Not only is the hand of the Lord upon you, my fellow
prisoners of hope, but because of the righteousness of
Jesus the Christ, you are in the palms of his hands.
"Behold, I have graven thee upon the palms of my
hands; thy walls are continually before me."
Can you see yourself liberated from all captivity
and embraced in God's mighty hands?

Yes _____

No _____

"Then was Daniel brought in before the king.
And the king spake and said unto Daniel, Art thou that
Daniel, which art of the children of the captivity of Judah,
whom the king my father brought out of Jewry?
Then answered they and said before the king, That
Daniel, which is of the children of the captivity of Judah,
regardeth not thee, O king, not the decree that thou hast
signed, but maketh his petition three times a day.
And they that understand among the people shall
instruct many, yet they shall fall by the sword, and by
flame, by captivity, and by spoil, many days."
Daniel 5:13; 6:13; 11:33

Manna:

Your relationship with Jesus will not diminish with you being
in captivity. It will only magnify, and set you apart. Having that
genuine connection with the Lord, and knowing you are under
His authority and power gives you confidence that captivity
or anything else cannot separate you from Him or His love.

Is Jesus your whole life?

Yes _____

No _____

"Also, O Judah, he hath set a harvest for thee, when

I returned the captivity of my people."

Hosea 6:11

Manna:

Break forth in joy and rejoicing, oh, prisoners of hope.

Your day of freedom is at hand. There is a light beaming at the

end of the tunnel, and it is not a freight train coming at you.

Jesus purchased your freedom on Calvary

over two thousand years ago.

Harvest your freedom now with shouts of

praise and break forth in a dance.

Do you receive Christ's freedom for you?

Yes _____

No _____

"For behold, in those days, and in that time, when I shall bring again the captivity of Judah and Jerusalem."

Joel 3:1

Manna:

Prisoners of hope, look, the replaying of "those days" are once again at hand. Prophesy does repeat itself at times, and this is one. God is setting men and women free from captivity of sin and imprisonment who call upon the name of Jesus for salvation. Are you a Christ-caller like blind Bartimaeus, who cried out, "Jesus, thou son of David, have mercy on me"?

Yes _____

No _____

"I will break also the bar of Damascus, and cut off the
inhabitant from the plain of Aven, and him that holdeth
the scepter from the house of Eden: and the people of
Syria shall go into captivity unto Kir, saith the Lord.
Thus saith the Lord; for three transgressions of Gaza, and for four,
I will not turn away the punishment thereof; because they carried
away captive the whole captivity, to deliver them up to them.
Thus saith the Lord; for three transgressions of Tyrus,
and for four I will not turn away the punishment
thereof; because they delivered up the whole captivity to
Edom, and remember not the brotherly covenant.
And their king shall go into captivity, he and
his princes together, saith the Lord."
Amos 1:5, 6, 9, 15

Manna:

Jesus gave His life on the cross to preserve the brotherly covenant,
and cut off the curse of sin and captivity from our lives.
Will you uphold God's love to others?

Yes _____

No _____

"But seek not Beth-el, nor enter into Gilgal, and
pass not to Beersheba: for Gilgal shall surely go into
captivity, and Bethel shall come to nought.
Therefore will I cause you to go into captivity beyond
Damascus, saith the Lord, whose name is The God of hosts.
Therefore thus saith the Lord; Thy wife shall be a harlot in the
city, and thy sons and thy daughters shall fall by the sword, and
thy land shall be divided by line; and thou shalt die in a polluted
land: and Israel shall surely go into captivity forth of his land."
Amos 5:5, 27; 7:17
Manna:
Whatever God told you to do, just do it. Your obedience
is the gateway for uncommon miracles, and preservation
and protection for you and your family from captivity.
"As for me and my house, we will serve the Lord."
Can you say the same thing too?
Yes _____
No _____

"And though they go into captivity before their enemies,
thence will I command the sword, and it shall slay them: and
I will set mine eyes upon them for evil, and not for good.
And I will bring again the captivity of my people of Israel,
and they shall build again waste cities, and inhabit them:
and they shall plant vineyards, and drink the wine thereof;
they shall also make gardens, and eat the fruit of them."

Amos 9:4, 14

Manna:

Without Jesus to come to our rescue captivity would have
strangled us alive. But with Jesus, we prisoners of hope
are armed with unshakeable hope and blessings from
God. He floods our lives and returns us from captivity
so we may rebuild our families in His Name.

Are you ready to lead by example for the Lord?

Yes _____

No _____

"And the captivity of the host of the children of
Israel shall possess that of the Canaanites, even unto
Zarephath: and the captivity of Jerusalem, which is in
Sepharad, shall possess the cities of the south."

Obadiah 20

Manna:

Lord Jesus, you possess our souls and our lives. We surrender all
to you who died to give us life, and life more abundantly. We
desire to possess nothing more than what you give. We are your
prisoners of hope. Our only aspiration is to do your will to the
glory of God the Father, and we are sure you have dismantled
the hold of captivity from our lives and future. Even as we are
standing out of captivity and in captivity awaiting our physical
freedom from captivity, nonetheless we are spiritually free.

Is your spirit free?

Yes _____

No _____

"Make thee bald, and poll thee for thy delicate children; enlarge thy baldness as the eagle; for they are gone into captivity from thee."

Micah 1:16

Manna:

No father with a heart can endure his children cattled away into captivity. The description of God's Word is grim but it is true.

God himself knows what it feels like as a Father, to have His innocent delicate Son offered up as a lamb, and slaughtered before His eyes on the cross of Calvary while being mocked by sinners. Yea, the whole world was gone into captivity. But His innocent death on the cross opened the flood gates of captivity for the world to be free, and your delicate children to return home.

Are you ready to celebrate Jesus?

He died but did you know He rose again?

Yes _____

No _____

"Yet was she carried away, she went into captivity: her young children also were dashed in pieces at the top of all the streets; and they cast lots for her honorable men, and all her great men were bound in chains."

Nahum 3:10

Manna:

Mothers have wept long enough over brutality, witnessing the death of their children. Their cries can be heard in heaven. The mother of God's only begotten Son, the virgin, and blessed mother Mary also wept as she witnessed the hands of cruel men tear her holy Son Jesus to pieces before nailing Him to that ugly cross between two thieves. Her cries also reached heaven, and the heart of her Son's Father Almighty God. Mothers, captivity is your enemy, but Jesus is your comfort and cure.

Will you let Him heal you?

Yes _____

No _____

"They shall come all for violence: their faces shall sup up as the east wind, and they shall gather the captivity as the sand."

Habakkuk 1:9

Manna:

Praise Jesus, who is the secret of your freedom from every dimension of captivity. His mercy is greater than any whirl-wind.

Will you praise Him?

Yes _____

No _____

"And the coast shall be for the remnant of the house of
Judah; they shall feed there upon: in the houses of Ashkelon
shall they lie down in the evening: for the Lord their
God shall visit them, and turn away their captivity.
At that time will I bring you again, even in the time
that I gather you: for I will make you a name and a
praise among all people of the earth, when I turn back
your captivity before your eyes, saith the Lord."

Zephaniah 2:7; 3:20

Manna:

God is big on reciprocity. He is huge on giving back to the
prisoners of hope in abundance for the sacrifices they give
to Him in offerings, and tithes in obedience to the faith.
Have you ever considered tithing your personal
prayers to pray for a lost sinner for a week?
He gave the life of His only begotten Son for the
sins of the world. And He will deliver on His Word
to bring you out of captivity in His time.
Did you know He has the wealth of the sinners laid up for you?

Yes _____

No _____

"Take of them of the captivity, even of Heldai, of Tobijah, and
of Jedaiah, which are come from Babylon, and come thou the
same day, and go into the house of Josiah the son of Zephaniah.
For I will gather all nations against Jerusalem to battle; and
the city shall be taken, and the houses rifled, and the women
ravished; and half of the city shall go forth into captivity, and
the residue of the people shall not be cut off from the city."

Zechariah 6:10; 14:2

Manna:

Never underestimate the power of God's grace given to you
in Jesus Christ for the safety of your soul, and your shield
against the jaws of captivity utterly consuming you.
God has gathered you safely under the covering of His Son, and
filled you with His Holy Spirit to guide and teach you in His way.

Do you count yourself one of His?

Yes _____

No _____

"But I see another law in my members, warring against
the law of my mind, and bringing me into captivity
to the law of sin which is in my members."

Romans 7:23

Manna:

Do not allow the law of sin and death to destroy you.
Let the law of grace liberate you, and give you life and peace in
Jesus who gave His life at Calvary for you. Become a prisoner of
hope today by receiving Jesus Christ into your heart right now.

Will you receive Him?

Yes _____

No _____

"Casting down imaginations, and every high thing that
exalteth itself against the knowledge of God, and bringing
into captivity every thought to the obedience of Christ."

2 Corinthians 10:5

Manna:

You have the choice of dismantling every defeating thought
that arises in your mind today, and you have the power of
the Holy Spirit in you as prisoners of hope to bring your life
in alignment to the obedience of God's holy Word today.

Will you do it today?

Yes _____

No _____

"Wherefore he saith, When he ascended up on high,

he led captivity captive, and gave gifts unto men."

Ephesians 4:8

"He that leadeth into captivity shall go into captivity: he

that killeth with the sword must be killed with the sword.

Here is the patience and the faith of the saints."

Revelation 13:10

Manna:

Jesus freed us from captivity when He led it captive to heaven.

He gave us gifts of empowerment, and loosed

us from death and imprisonment.

Yes, He looseth the prisoners of hope.

Do you agree?

Yes _____

No _____

CHAPTER 8

Hope

"Then again, my daughter, go your way; for I am too old
to have a husband, if I should say, I have hope, if I should
have a husband also to night, and should also bear."

Ruth 1:12

"And Shechaniah the son of Jehiel, one of the sons of Elam,
answered and said unto Ezra, We have trespassed against our
God, and have taken strange wives of the people of the land:
yet now there is hope in Israel concerning this thing."

Ezra 10:2

Manna:

Hope is smiling at the future with confidence, knowing
that God's promises must come to pass in your life.

Amen!

"Is not this thy fear, thy confidence, thy hope;

and the uprightness of thy ways?

So the poor hath hope, and iniquity stoppeth her mouth.

What is my strength, that I should hope?

And what is mine end, that I should prolong my life?

My days are swifter than a weaver's shuttle.

And are spent without hope.

So are the paths of all that forget God; and

the hypocrite's hope shall perish.

Whose hope shall be cut off, and whose

trust shall be a spider's web."

Job 4:6; 5:16; 6:11; 7:6; 8:13–14

Manna:

Hope is enlarging your imagination to dream of the bright

future beyond these walls in Christ Jesus awaiting you.

Amen!

"And thou shalt be secure, because there is hope; yea, thou

shalt dig about thee, and thou shalt take thy rest in safety.

But the eyes of the wicked shall fail, and they shall not escape,

and their hope shall be as the giving up of the ghost.

For there is hope of a tree, if it be cut down, that it will sprout

again, and that the tender branch thereof will not cease.

The waters wear the stones: thou washest away the

things which grow out of the dust of the earth;

and thou destroyed the hope of man."

Job 11:18, 20; 14:7, 19

Manna:

No longer shall your hope be shattered, you prisoners of hope.

In Christ Jesus, your hope is alive and sure.

Amen!

"And where is now my hope? As for my hope, who shall see it?

He hath destroyed me on every side, and I am gone:

and mine hope hath he removed like a tree.

For what is the hope of the hypocrite, though he

hath gained, when God taketh away his soul?

If I have made gold my hope, or have said to

the fine gold, thou art my confidence.

Behold, the hope of him is in vain: shall not one

be cast down even at the sight of him."

Job 17:15; 19:10; 27:8; 31:24; 41:9

Manna:

Declare the testimony of your heart to the world

that your hope is in Jesus Christ who gives freedom

to all prisoners who dare to believe in Him.

Amen!

"Therefore my heart is glad, and my glory
rejoiceth: my flesh also shall rest in hope.
But thou art he that took me out of the womb: thou didst
make me hope when I was upon my mother's breasts.
Be of good courage, and he shall strengthen
your heart, all ye that hope in the Lord."
Psalm 16:9; 22:9; 31:24

Manna:

Prevail in hope, all you prisoners of hope.

Amen!

"Behold, the eye of the Lord is upon them that fear
him, upon them that hope in his mercy.
Let thy mercy, O Lord, be upon us according as we hope in thee.
For in thee, O Lord, do I hope: thou wilt hear, O Lord my God.
And now, Lord, what wait I for? my hope is in thee."
Psalm 33:18, 22; 38:15; 39:7
Manna:
Prisoners of hope, never allow your hope for freedom to diminish.
Amen!

"Why art thou cast down, O my soul? and why are
thou disquieted in me? hope thou in God: for I shall
yet praise him for the help of his countenance.
Why art thou cast down, O my soul? and why art thou
disquieted within me? hope thou in God: for I shall yet praise
him, who is the health of my countenance, and my God.
Why art thou cast down, O my soul? and why art thou
disquieted within me? hope in God: for I shall yet praise
him who is the health of my countenance, and my God."
Psalm 42:5, 11; 43:5

Manna:

Prisoners of hope, fire up the eternal hope of God in your spirits.

Amen!

"For thou art my hope, O Lord God: thou
art my trust from my youth.
But I will hope continually, and will yet praise thee more and more.
That they might set their hope in God, and not forget
the works of God, but keep his commandments."
Psalm 71:5, 14; 78:7
Manna:
Engross your mind masterfully in the hope of glory, which is
Christ Jesus, the key for every prisoner of hope's freedom.
Amen!

"Remember the word unto thy servant, upon
which thou hast caused me to hope.
My soul fainteth for thy salvation: but I hope in thy word.
Thou art my hiding place and my shield: I hope in thy word.
Uphold me according unto thy word, that I may
live: and let me not be ashamed of my hope."
Psalm 119:49, 81, 114, 116
Manna:
Hope is a powerful Niagara of supernatural, spiritual
force flowing into the lives of every prisoner of hope.
Amen!

"I wait for the Lord, my soul doth wait, and in his word do I hope.

Let Israel hope in the Lord: for with the Lord there is

mercy, and with him is plenteous redemption.

Happy is he that hath the God of Jacob for his

help, whose hope is in the Lord his God.

The Lord taketh pleasure in them that fear

him, in those that hope in his mercy."

Psalm 130:5, 7; 146:5; 147:11

Manna:

Once you activate the hope of Christ in

your life it cannot be turned off.

Amen!

"The hope of the righteous shall be gladness: but
the expectation of the wicked shall perish.
When a wicked man dieth, his expectation shall
perish: and the hope of unjust men perisheth.
Hope deferred maketh the heart sick: but when
the desire cometh, it is a tree of life.
The wicked is driven away in his wickedness: but
the righteous hath hope in his death."
Proverbs 10:28; 11:7; 13:12; 14:32
Manna:
Hope makes you shine through the darkness
of adversity bright as stars.
Amen!

"Chasten thy son while there is hope, and let

not thy soul spare for his crying.

Seest thou a man wise in his own conceit? there

is more hope of a fool than of him.

Seest thou a man that is hasty in his word? there

is more hope of a fool than of him."

Proverbs 19:18; 26:12; 29:20

Manna:

Hope is like a volcano eruption blazing with piercing

power from the depth of the ocean floor.

It cannot stop by any means in the prisoner of hope's lives.

Amen!

"For to him that is joined to all the living there is hope: for a living dog is better than a dead lion."

Ecclesiastes 9:4

Manna:

Hope gives strength in darkness to the prisoners of hope.

Amen!

"For the grave cannot praise thee, death cannot celebrate thee:
they that go down into the pit cannot hope for thy truth.
Thou art wearied in the greatness of the way; yet saidst
thou not, there is no hope: thou hast found the life
of thine hand; therefore thou wast not grieved."

Isaiah 38:18; 57:10

Manna:

When a prisoner takes hope in Christ, he
finds the key to his freedom.

Amen!

"Withhold thy foot from being unshod, and thy throat
from thirst: but thou saidst, There is no hope: no; for
I have loved strangers, and after them will I go.
O the hope of Israel, the savior thereof in time of trouble,
why shouldest thou be as a stranger in thy land, and as a
wayfaring man that turneth aside to tarry for a night?"
Jeremiah 2:25; 4:8
Manna:
Hope in Christ Jesus breaks the chains
that bind the prisoners of hope.
Amen!

"Blessed is the man that trusteth in the

Lord, and whose hope the Lord is.

O Lord, the hope of Israel, all that forsake thee shall be ashamed,

and they that depart from me shall be written in the earth, because

they have forsaken the Lord, the fountain of living waters.

Be not a terror unto me: thou art my hope in the day of evil."

Jeremiah 17:7, 13, 17

Manna:

Oh, prisoners of hope, your hope is governed

by God but directed by you.

Amen!

"And they said, There is no hope: but we will walk after our own
devices, and we will everyone do the imagination of his evil heart.
And there is hope in thine end, saith the Lord, that thy
children shall come again to their own border.
All that found them have devoured them: and their adversaries
said, We offend not, because they have sinned against the Lord,
the habitation of justice, even the Lord, the hope of their father."
Jeremiah 18:12; 31:17; 50:7
Manna:
Hope triggers the impossible to possibility for the
prisoners of hope, and cracks open wide the doors
of the habitation of injustice in every country.
Amen!

"And I said, My strength and my hope is perished from the Lord.

This I recall to my mind, therefore have I hope.

The Lord is my portion, saith my soul; therefore will I hope in him.

It is good that a man should both hope and

quietly wait for the salvation of the Lord.

He putteth his mouth in the dust; if so be there may be hope."

Lamentations 3:18, 21, 24, 26, 29

Manna:

Preserve your spirit, soul, mind, and body with

the helmet of salvation that is Hope. Be proactive,

prisoners of hope. We have a lively hope.

Amen!

"They have seen vanity and lying divination, saying, the Lord saith: and the Lord hath not sent them: and they have made others to hope that they would confirm the word. Now when she saw that she had waited, and her hope was lost, then she took another of her whelps, and made him a young lion. Then he said unto me, Son of man, these bones are the whole house of Israel: behold, they say, Our bones are dried, and our hope is lost: we are cut off for our parts."

Ezekiel 13:6; 19:5; 37:11

Manna:

Your hope in Jesus is able to resuscitate even that hopeless, dead, dried situation you thought was overly impossible.

Amen!

"And I will give her her vineyards from thence, and the valley of Achor for a door of hope: and she shall sing there, as in the days of her youth, and as in the day when she came up out of the land of Egypt."

Hosea 2:15

"The Lord also shall roar out of Zion, and utter his voice from Jerusalem; and the heavens and the earth shall shake: but the Lord will be the hope of his people, and the strength of the children of Israel."

Joel 3:16

"Turn ye to the strong hold, ye prisoners of hope; even today do I declare that I will render double unto you."

Zechariah 9:12

Manna:

Hope kept the doors of freedom open for you, prisoners of hope.

Amen!

"And if you lend to them of whom ye hope to receive, what thank have ye? for sinners also lend to sinners, to receive as much again."

Luke 6:34

"Therefore did my heart rejoice, and my tongue was glad; moreover also my flesh shall rest in hope."

Acts 2:26

"And when her masters saw that the hope of their gains was gone, they caught Paul and Silas, and drew them into the market-place unto the rulers."

Acts 16:19

Manna:

Prisoners of hope, there is a lively hope for us to be found in Jesus Christ that can never die.

Amen!

"But when Paul perceived that the one part were Sadducees,
and the other Pharisees, he cried out in the council, Men and
brethren, I am a Pharisee, the son of a Pharisee of the hope
and resurrection of the dead I am called into question."

Acts 23:6

"And have hope towards God, which they themselves
also allow, that there shall be a resurrection of
the dead, both of the just and unjust."

Acts 24:15

"And now I stand and am judged for the hope of
the promise made of God unto our fathers."

Acts 26:6

Manna:

Hope is the prisoner of hope's most valued
weapon against the army of fear.

Amen!

"Unto which promise our twelve tribes, instantly serving
God day and night, hope to come, For which hope's
sake, king Agrippa, I am accused of the Jews."

Acts 26:7

"And when neither sun nor stars in many days
appeared, and no small tempest lay on us, all hope
that we should be saved was then taken away."

Acts 27:20

"For this cause therefore have I called for you, to
see you, and to speak with you: because that for the
hope of Israel I am bound with this chain."

Acts 28:20

Manna:

Under the covenant of Christ, all prisoners of hope
are bound to a fixed hope never to fail or perish.

Amen!

"Who against hope believed in hope, that he might

become the father of many nations; according to

that which was spoken, So shall thy seed be."

Romans 4:18

"By whom also we have access by faith into this grace wherein

we stand, and rejoice in hope of the glory of God.

And patience, experience; and experience, hope.

And hope maketh not ashamed; because the love of God is shed

abroad in our hearts by the Holy Ghost which is given unto us."

Romans 5:2–5

Manna:

Hope unashamedly cements the expectation

of every prisoner of hope.

Amen!

"For the creature was made subject to vanity, not willingly,

but by reason of him who hath subjected the same in hope.

For we are saved by hope: but that is seen is not hope:

for what a man seeth, why doth he yet hope for?

But if we hope for that we see not, then

do we with patience wait for it."

Romans 8:20, 24, 25

Manna:

We prisoners of hope are created by God to be subjected to hope.

Amen!

"Rejoicing in hope; patient in tribulation;
continuing instant in prayer.
For whatsoever things were written aforetime were
written for our learning, that we through patience
and comfort of the scriptures might have hope.
Now the God of hope fill you with all joy and
peace in believing, that ye may abound in hope,
through the power of the Holy Ghost."
Romans 12:12; 15:4, 13
Manna:
Your attitude toward hope determines the environment
you coin for your freedom and future. Remember
these words: "Now the God of hope . . ."
Amen!

"Or saith he it altogether for our sakes? For our sake, no doubt,

this is written: that he that ploweth should plow in hope; and

that he that thresheth in hope should be partaker of his hope.

And now abideth faith, hope, charity, these

three; but the greatest of these is charity.

If in this life only we have hope in Christ,

we are of all men most miserable."

1 Corinthians 9:10; 13:13; 15:19

Manna:

Believe in hope, pray in hope, plow in hope, sow in hope,

wait in hope, walk in hope, rest in hope, and sleep in

hope, and as prisoners of hope, you will reap in hope.

Amen!

"And our hope of you is steadfast, knowing, that as you are
partakers of the sufferings, so shall ye be also of the consolation.
Seeing then that we have such hope, we
use great plainness of speech.
Not boasting of things without our measure, that is, of other
men's labors, but having hope, when your faith is increased, that
we shall be enlarged by you according to our rule abundantly."
2 Corinthians 1:7; 3:12; 10:15
Manna:
There is no limitation to what hope can bring about
in the lives of faithful prisoners of hope.
Do not quit!
Amen!

"For we through the Spirit wait for the
hope of righteousness by faith."
Galatians 5:5
"The eyes of your understanding being enlightened: that
ye may know what is the hope of his calling, and what
the riches of the glory of his inheritance in the saint.
That at that time ye were without Christ, being aliens from
the commonwealth of Israel, and strangers from the covenants
of promise, having no hope, and without God in the word.
There is one body, and one Spirit, even as you
are called in one hope of your calling."
Ephesians 1:8; 2:12; 4:4
Manna:
Once you discover the strength of hope, you
conquered life as prisoners of hope.
Amen!

"According to my earnest expectation and my hope,
that in nothing I shall be ashamed, but that with all
boldness, as always, so now also Christ shall be magnified
in my body, whether it be by life, or by death.
Him therefore I hope to send presently, so soon
as I shall see how it will go with me."
Philippians 1:20; 2:3
Manna:
Hope springs from the throne of God, and flows into the
hearts of every prisoner of hope with supernatural boldness
proclaiming the victory of Christ's life in them. Freedom!
Amen!

"For the hope which is laid up for you in heaven, whereof
ye heard before in the word of the truth of the gospel.
If ye continue in the faith grounded and settled, and be not
moved away from the hope of the gospel, which ye have
heard, and which was preached to every creature which
is under heaven; whereof I Paul am made a minister.
To whom God would make known what is the riches
of the glory of this mystery among the Gentiles;
which is Christ in you, the hope of glory."
Colossians 1:5, 23, 27

Manna:

Truly, hope will enhance your quality of life.
Prisoners of hope, be hopeful! Walk in hope; live in hope.

Amen!

"Remembering without ceasing your work of faith,
and labor of love, and patience of hope in our Lord
Jesus Christ, in the sight of God and our Father.
For what is our hope, or joy or crown of rejoicing? Are not even
ye in the presence of our Lord Jesus Christ at his coming.
But I would not have you to be ignorant, brethren
concerning them which are asleep, that ye sorrow
now, even as others which have no hope.
But let us, who are of the day, be sober, putting on the breastplate
of faith and love; and for a helmet, the hope of salvation."
1 Thessalonians 1:3; 2:19; 4:13; 5:8
Manna:
Hope refines the spirit of the downcast with quiet confidence.
Amen!

"Now our Lord Jesus Christ himself, and God, even our Father, which hath loved us, and hath given us everlasting consolation and good hope through grace."

2 Thessalonians 2:16

"Paul, an apostle of Jesus Christ by the commandment of God our Savior, and Lord Jesus Christ, which is our hope."

1 Timothy 1:1

Manna:

Having seized upon the good hope that our loving Father has bestowed upon us, we as prisoners of hope are inspired to let others see Christ in us.

Amen!

"In hope of eternal life, which God, that cannot
lie, promised before the world began.
Looking for that blessed hope, and the glorious appearing
of the great God and our Savior Jesus Christ.
That being justified by his grace, we should be made
heirs according to the hope of eternal life."
Titus 1:2; 2:13; 3:7
Manna:
Hope is an eternal force in which God wrapped His
character, and gives to us prisoners of hope as a sure door
of access from the prison cell to freedom and eternity.
Amen!

"But Christ as a Son over his own house; whose
house are we, if we hold fast the confidence and
the rejoicing of the hope firm unto the end.
And we desire that every one of you do shew the same
diligence to the full assurance of hope unto the end.
That by two immutable things, in which it was impossible
for God to lie, we might have a strong consolation, who have
fled for refuge to lay hold upon the hope set before us.
Which hope we have as an anchor of the soul, both sure and
steadfast, and which entereth into that within the vail."
Hebrews 3:6; 6:11, 18–19

Manna:

In the midst of the storm, hope anchors the
prisoners of hope until the end.

Amen!

"For the law made nothing perfect, but the bringing in of a better hope did; by that which we draw nigh unto God."

Hebrews 7:19

Manna:

Hope is a magnetic field that draws the prisoners of hope's attention to the presence of God and to the realization that the holy God will work out all things for the good.

Amen!

"Blessed be the God and Father of our Lord Jesus Christ, which according to his abundant mercy hath begotten us again unto a lively hope by the resurrection of Jesus Christ from the dead. Who by him do believe in God, that raised him up from the dead, and gave him glory; that your faith and hope might be in God. But sanctify the Lord God in your hearts: and be ready always to give an answer to every man that asketh you a reason of the hope that is in you with meekness and fear."

1 Peter 1:3, 21; 3:15

Manna:

Hope expresses bold confessions of the indicatives and imperatives the prisoners of hope take hold of in God's Word.

Amen!

"And every man that hath this hope in him
purifieth himself, even as he is pure."

1 John 3:3

Manna:

A pure heart is evidence of genuine hope for prisoners of hope.

Amen!

"Now in the twelfth month, that is, the month Adar, on the thirteenth day of the same, when the king's commandment and his decree drew near to be put in execution, in the day that the enemies of the Jews hoped to have power over them, though it was turned to the contrary, that the Jews had rule over them that hated them."

Esther 9:1

Manna:

Do not panic under the pressure of imprisonment. Be a prisoner of hope. All you need is hope in Christ, and God Almighty will turn the table for you.

Amen!

"What is my strength, that I should hope? and what
is my end, that I should prolong my life?
They were confounded because they had hope;
they came thither, and were ashamed."

Job 6:11, 20

Manna:

Hope is like a defibrillator to the prisoners of hope who once were
dying under the weight of mountains of despair with shattered lives.

Amen!

"And take not the word of truth utterly out of
my mouth; for I hoped in thy judgment.
They that fear thee will be glad when they
see me; because I hope in thy word.
I prevented the dawning of the morning,
and cried: I hoped in thy word.
Lord, I have hoped for thy salvation, and
done thy commandments."
Psalm 119: 43, 74, 147, 166
Manna:
The Word of God is the foundation of the prisoners of hope.
Hope in Jesus.
Amen!

"Truly in vain is salvation hoped for from the hills, and from the multitude of mountains: truly in the Lord our God is the salvation of Israel."

Jeremiah 3:23

Manna:

Prisoners of hope, it is truly vain to lock and load your hope in the strength of any other than Jesus Christ the Author and Finisher of our salvation.

Amen!

"And when Herod saw Jesus, he was exceedingly glad: for he was desirous to see him of a long season, because he heard many things of him; and he hoped to have seen some miracle done by him."

Luke 23:8

"He hoped also that money should have been given him of Paul, that he might lose him: wherefore he sent for him the oftener, and communed with him."

Acts 24:26

Manna:

The power of hope will take a prisoner of hope from the impossible to an earthquake of miracles.

Amen!

"And this they did, not as we hoped, but first gave their own selves to the Lord, and unto us by the will of God."

2 Corinthians 8:5

"Now faith is the substance of things hoped for, the evidence of things not seen."

Hebrews 11:1

Manna:

Prisoners of hope, it takes a conscious decision for your eyes to be opened and your mind prepared to receive with the hands of faith the gifts freely given by God in Christ.

Amen!

"Unto which promise our twelve tribes, instantly
serving God day and night, hope to come.
For which hope's sake king Agrippa, I am accused of the Jews."

Acts 26:7

Manna:

Lift up your heads.

The promise of hope cannot fail, fade, or die. It is
heaven's eternal hope, given to redeem men and women
on this earth who say "Yes" to Jesus for salvation.

Amen!

"Beareth all things, believeth all things, hopeth
all things, endureth all things."
1 Corinthians 13:7
Manna:
The scale of human injustice cannot bend the
expectations or faith of the prisoner of hope.
The resurrection hopeth all things.
The power of Jesus Christ burneth deep within their
souls as a wildfire that cannot be quenched.
Amen!

"We have also a more sure word of prophecy; whereunto ye do well that ye take heed, as unto a light that shineth in a dark place, until the day dawn, and the day star arises in your hearts."

2 Peter 1:19

The beginning

of your

freedom!

"Thanks be unto God for his unspeakable *gift*."

2 Corinthians 9:15

Sinner's Prayer

Lord Jesus, my heart is open unto you, and your love.

I know you are the Son of God.

I know you died for my sins, and rose again
on the third day to give me a new life.

I accept you into my heart, as my Lord and personal savior.

Fill me with your Holy Spirit.

Holy Spirit, I receive you right now in Jesus Name.

Thank You Father.

Amen!

Christ's Liberation of Grace

My incarceration has become my liberation, because life's
interpretation has totally changed beyond leaps and bounds.
It is as if my miseducation versus my education has gotten my mind
going through a metamorphosis.
Time can heal my broken heart; Angie is eternally gone, but
through my trials and tribulations my concepts of real is humility
followed by God's grace.
I heard, "Knowledge is key" so without "knowledge" of God how
can we save this generation?
Solitude in a six-by-five-feet prison cell changed my attitude with
one touch from Jesus.
Now my power comes in the form of a book.
Personal gratification comes in the Man, Christ Jesus.
The Proverb goes, "A righteous man falls seven times and rises up
again."
Work hard to be a man.
The lesson you learn will shape the man.
Prison can be a gift or a curse.

I chose to use mine evolving through time, because time allows me to reach for true freedom in Christ. So every second I am alive, I embrace the essence of my existence.

Realistically speaking, freedom must be embraced mentally and spiritually before obtaining anything.

Reality today versus reality yesterday, is separated by intelligence versus stupidity.

I am a new man.

To be new is to be different.

So consider me a rarity.

I am not the man I used to be.

Respect is not validated by how many people know you, but by who knows you, and how many people you are willing to show that life consists of transitional changes every day. So as I bring this book to a poetic halt, I appeal to all my fellow men and women deprived of liberty, to seek true freedom in Jesus Christ.

A prisoner of hope's, final word sealing the end of this book.

About the Author

Newton R. Francis

- A solitarily confined vessel, and prisoner of hope.
- Under heavy spiritual adjustment for
the Lord Jesus Christ's service.
- Having been purged of all my sins, and stripped of all
worldly desires—no longer to compete on the world's stage.
- Writing from a tiny prison cell in some
dark corner of the great USA
- Locked away from family and society.
- A lover of Jesus Christ and the family who obeys Him.
A father and grandfather.
To my sons and daughters, I love you all dazzlingly dearly.
Father, it is me again!
Glory to your Holy Name.
I love you, Holy Spirit.
You are the best thing that is ever happened to me.
Thanks!
Amen!

CPSIA information can be obtained
at www.ICGtesting.com
Printed in the USA
LVHW032223010722
722610LV00001B/66

9 781641 403702